STUDIES IN HISTORY, ECONOMICS AND PUBLIC LAW

Edited by the

**FACULTY OF POLITICAL SCIENCE
OF COLUMBIA UNIVERSITY**

NUMBER 424

VIKING ENTERPRISE

BY

SVEN AXEL ANDERSON

VIKING ENTERPRISE

SVEN AXEL ANDERSON

AMS Press, Inc.
New York
1966

To

THE MEMORY OF

I. I. A.

PREFACE

THE purpose of the present study is to elucidate in a realistic way the viking traffic and possibly contribute a chapter to economic history.

My interest in the viking traffic and my decision to attempt an interpretation of it is in good part due to a number of comments on the activities of the Swedes in Russia in viking times by Professor Vladimir G. Simkhovitch. I am further indebted to Professor Simkhovitch for stimulating advice during the preparation of the study. I owe a great debt of gratitude to Dr. Joseph Dorfman, Columbia University, for his thorough criticism and numerous suggestions, especially with regard to the organization of the material. Professor John H. Wuorinen, Columbia University, gave me much valuable advice in matters pertaining to Scandinavian history. My appreciation is also extended to Professors Leo Wolman and Arthur R. Burns, Columbia University and Dr. Robert L. Sharp, Wheaton College, who have read the manuscript. Miss Harriet Peck, Librarian of Rensselear Polytechnic Institute, has aided me greatly in making available a number of necessary books.

S. A. A.

TROY, NEW YORK
JUNE, 1936.

CONTENTS

CHAPTER I

INTRODUCTION

THE era of viking domination of the economic life of a great part of Northwestern Europe and Western Russia is generally referred to as the viking age.[1] This age, as a distinct period in European history, may be said to begin with the attacks by the Northmen upon Lindisfarne and Jarrow toward the end of the eighth century and to close about the middle of the eleventh century.[2] With a varying degree of intensity, this period was marked by unprecedented piratical and marauding activities in England, France, on the shores of the Mediterranean and in Russia. But sporadic attacks had been common for centuries prior to the advent of the viking age.[3] Since the time of Caesar, the

---

[1] The most commonly accepted explanation of the origin of the term "viking" is that it is derived from "*vik*," an Old Norse word for bay, still used in the present day Norwegian and Swedish. It is the contention that the rovers of the North received their name from the fact that the base of their operations was invariably situated in such a "*vik*" or landlocked and placid inlet or bay. *Cf.* Johannes C. H. R. Steenstrup, *Normannerne* (Copenhagen, 1876-1878), vol. iv, pp. 162-163; Fridtjof Nansen, *In Northern Mists* (New York, 1911), vol. i, p. 224; A. Bugge, *Norges Historie* (Oslo, 1909), *Bind* i, *Del* 2, p. 71; and T. D. Kendrick, *A History of the Vikings* (London, 1911), p. 2. (Oslo, formerly Christiania, is indicated as the place of publication even where the title page bears the latter name.

[2] The monastery of Lindisfarne was situated on the Holy Island and that of Jarrow a few miles further south, both on the North Sea coast of England.

[3] See Oscar Montelius, "Sveriges förbindelser med andra länder i förhistorisk tid," in *Festskrift tillägnad C. G. Malmström* (Stockholm,

Northmen, as well as the peoples immediately to the south of them, had launched attacks upon various parts of Europe. Tacitus describes the Swedes as being powerful in the Baltic because of their " men, weapons and fleets." The Northmen also played a role in the *Völkerwanderungen,* as is shown by the references to the *Eruli.* The latter tribe once sent to Thule for a leader, and a contingent of them is said to have " returned home to Gothaland." These earlier activities, however, never attained the size and intensity that characterized the operations of the viking period proper.

The vikings came from the North, more particularly from the regions which now include the kingdoms of Sweden, Denmark, Norway and Iceland.   Only in a general way is it possible to localize the field of operation of the various nationalities concerned.   It appears that the Swedes concentrated their efforts on the East Baltic, Russia, Constantinople and the Near East, the Danes on the Carolingian Empire and England, and the Norwegians focused their attention on Ireland, Scotland and a number of other parts of the West.[4]   But people from any one of the regions of

1897), pp. 16-22; Kaspar Zeus, *Die Deutschen und die Nachbarstämme* (Munich, 1837), p. 447; Karl Mullenhoff, *Beovulf* (Berlin, 1889), p. 19; and R. E. M. Wheeler, *London Museum Catalogues,* no. 1 (1927), p. 7.

[4] The terms " Swedes," " Danes " and " Norwegians " are here used to designate the peoples of the approximate regions that now constitute Sweden, Denmark and Norway. Except for the district of Scania in the south and Viken, the region west of Lake Vänern, Sweden included almost all of its present day territory. Sweden contained a number of independent units, each governed according to its own laws. However, these units acted together in time of need, and appear to have recognized the rule of a single king after the eighth century (Birger Nerman, *Det svenska rikets uppkomst,* Stockholm, 1925, p. 266). The accounts of Othere and Wulfstan, in conjunction with King Alfred's own observations, show that in the beginning of the viking period Denmark was divided into two states: one occupying Jutland, and the other comprising Zealand, the islands and Scania (Alfred the Great, *A Description of Europe and the Voyages of Othere and Wulfstan,* Bosworth's ed., Lon-

the North mentioned above, sought their fortune also where Northmen from other parts held sway, either independently or in conjunction with them. " Ulf had three times collected tribute in England," states a runic inscription on a stone near Orkesta parish church in Uppland, Sweden. Another Swedish rune-stone at Högby in Östergötland bears the following inscription:

> Five sons begot Gulle,
> a farmer good.
> At Fyris fell Åsmund,
> unafraid warrior.
> Atsur succumbed
> in East in Greece.
> Halvdan was
> in Bornholm slain,
> Kåre at Dundee,
> and dead is Boe.[5]

In the Irish and the English chronicles the terms generally applied to the vikings are *Dani* and *Normanni* or *Northmanni*. The majority of the vikings in the West were Danes and Norwegians, but the records show that there were also Swedes among them. It is said about the Byzantine Varangians, who were predominantly Swedes, that " the people whom the Greeks call *Russi* are by others called *Nor-*

don, 1855). *Cf.* Kendrick, *op. cit.*, p. 94. It was not until the tenth century that Harald Gormsson brought all Denmark under his rule. See Erik Arup, *Danmarks Historie* (Copenhagen, 1925), vol. i, pp. 122 *et seq.* Periodically, Vestfold and other parts of Norway may have been controlled by Denmark. See *Einhardi Annales* (ed. G. H. Pertz, *Monumenta Germaniae Historica, Scriptores*, Hanover, 1826, vol. ii, p. 200) ; *cf.* Kendrick, *op. cit.*, p. 94, note 2. At the dawn of the viking era, Norway was divided into a number of districts or states. The unification was effected by Harald Fairhair at the turn of the ninth and tenth centuries. The district of Viken belonged to Norway.

[5] The last line suggests that Boe merely died a natural death. Fyris is a river in Uppland, Sweden, near which a famous battle took place.

manni, because of the location of their homeland." [6]   An
Icelander was a captain in the Emperor's Guard at Constantinople, and there were also Norwegians and Danes in large
numbers among the Northmen in the East.[7]

The viking activities dominated an epoch in the history
of Northwestern Europe and Russia.   This study has for
its purpose to shed some light upon the character of these
activities.   Any attempt to understand the viking movement
requires first of all a consideration of the material conditions and the institutions of the North itself.[8]

[6] *Liudprand, Works,* v, 6.   The Varangians were the members of the
Emperor's Guard at Constantinople.   The term was also applied to the
Northmen in Russia.   See *The Russian Primary Chronicle.*

[7] *Saga of Burnt Nial,* 32; *Saxo Grammaticus* (J. Olrik's transl., iii-iv,
p. 41).   For a spirited discussion of the nationality of the participants in
the viking enterprises, see Steenstrup, *op. cit.,* vol. ii, pp. 13-14; Gustav
Storm, *Kritiske bidrag til vikingetidens historie* (Oslo, 1878), pp. 182-
191 and *Norsk Hist. Tidskrift, 2 Række, 2 Bind* (1881), pp. 271-293.
Steenstrup maintained that the vikings in England and France were almost entirely Danes while Storm pointed out that many of them unquestionably came from Norway.

[8] Since I have made considerable use of the saga material in my attempt
to describe the institutions of the North, it may be proper at this juncture
to offer a few comments on their historical reliability.

The saga literature, with a few exceptions, originated in Iceland, but
drew its impulses from the Scandinavian North as a whole.   The events
that the sagas depict, insofar as they are historical, took place in the
years from about 930 to about 1030 (Knut Liestol, *The Origin of the
Icelandic Family Saga,* Oslo, 1930, p. 25).   During the eleventh century, these events, historical and fictitious, crystallized into a tradition
which for several centuries was told and retold to succeeding generations.   Most of the sagas were committed to parchment during the period
from about 1120 to about 1230.   The oldest written saga known, the
Saga of Saint Olav, was written down in Iceland probably about the
year 1160 (Halvdan Koht, *The Old Norse Sagas,* New York, 1931,
pp. 36-49; Liestol, *op. cit.,* p. 49).

Liestol states that "the sagas are our most important sources of information regarding the history of Iceland during the period of more than
a hundred years; and the information they contain regarding life and

customs of those times is of immense historical value for the study, not only to Iceland, but of Scandinavian and even German culture" (*op. cit.*, p. 182). The sagas are, says Halvdan Koht, "always balancing between fiction and history, and one can never decide *a priori* to which the balance may gravitate." But in spite of the large fictional element in them, they still contain enough facts which "alone permit us to write the history of centuries" (*op. cit.*, pp. 138-139). G. Gathorne-Hardy believes that "it is a mistake to classify saga as fiction." Commenting upon the many unquestionably incredible incidents and details surrounding the story of Erling Skalgson and the administration of his estate found in the *Saga of Saint Olav*, Gathorne-Hardy states that . . . "yet the whole story may be said to be really truer than truth; it brings before the reader, in unforgettable form, the essential clash of interests which characterized this reign" (*Norway*, London, 1925, p. 139).

No historical structure can be built with the material which the Old Norse literature has to offer. But when the sagas are used in combination with the provincial law codes, runic inscriptions and the non-Scandinavian literary sources dealing with the North, a picture of the Northmen and their mode of making a living may be obtained.

CHAPTER II

MATERIAL BACKGROUND

LONG before the period of intensive exploitation abroad, as well as during that period, the Northmen dwelt in the northern lands, deriving a living from agriculture, fishing and hunting. In the viking age proper, we find that some of them were engaged in trade, to augment the returns derived from piracy and plunder; others followed trade as a primary occupation, but their number, relatively speaking, does not appear to have been great.[1] With the exception of the outlaws, who chose inaccessible cliff-islands for their headquarters, the viking entrepreneurs, marauders as well as traders, lived on their estates or homesteads in the winter or when not traveling about pursuing their business. Even the famous merchants of Gotland resided on estates located inland, a distance away from the shore or trading towns, and came to the latter only on specifically designated days for commerce.[2] Only Hedeby-Slesvik and Birka had a resident population living solely from trade. Hedeby-Slesvik, however, was predominantly a Frisian town, and in Birka, a large part of the population was likewise Frisian.[3]

[1] W. Vogel, *Geschichte der deutschen Seeschiffahrt* (Berlin, 1915), p. 99.

[2] A. Schück, *Fornvännen, 1924*, p. 17.

[3] That Birka was of Frisian origin and inhabited chiefly by Frisians was first suggested by Knut Stjerna (*Historisk Tidskrift för Skåneland, iii, 1909*, pp. 176 et seq.), who based his conclusions upon the archaeological finds. See, however, H. Schück. *Birka* (Upsala, 1910), pp. 1-29 and Sven Tunberg, *Studier rörande Skandinaviens äldsta politiska indelning*, (Upsala, 1911), p. 198.

AGRICULTURE

The basic society of the Northmen was one of landed proprietors.[4] It was the custom that the young men should serve a sort of *Wanderjahr* in far-off places as marauders, as Varangians in the East, and occasionally as traders. Approaching middle age, or even earlier in life, most vikings retired to become country squires or to enter the service of landed men. But few of the estates were sufficiently large to permit the former vikings to maintain their accustomed standard of living. Old Kettil, one of the saga personages, is said to have reminded his indifferent and lackadaisical son Thorstein that " in the past it was the custom among prominent men, kings, jarls, and other equals of ours to fare a-viking in order to acquire honor and riches. The wealth thus accumulated was generally not passed on from father to son, but was placed in the mound with the owner himself. Even if the sons inherited their father's possessions, they were unable to maintain the estates unless they took part in an expedition overseas now and then." [5] Likewise, Erling Skalgson, the brother-in-law of King Olav, " was often out in summer on plundering expeditions, and procured for himself means of living; for he continued his usual way of high and splendid living, although he had fewer and less certain land rents than in the days of King Olav, his Kinsman." [6]

---

[4] The word "*allmoge*" which in modern Swedish denotes the agrarian class meant originally "the whole group" or "the people," and in the evolution of the meaning of this word alone, one may see a reason for believing that the farmers or the cultivators of the soil at one time constituted the entire population of Sweden (H. Hildebrand, *Sveriges medeltid*, Stockholm, 1879, vol. i, p. 63).

[5] Joh. A. Enander, *Våra fäders sinnelag: fornnordiska karaktersdrag tecknade efter den isländska sagolitteraturen* (Stockholm, 1894), p. 86.

[6] *Heimskringla, Saga of Saint Olav*, 2.

In Sweden the land was divided into towns and neighborhoods, and single farms or estates. No neighborhoods or villages were found in Norway; each family lived on its own estate.[7] The village had for its nucleus the cultivated fields of the various farmers with their homes and barns. Outside were other fields and pastures belonging to the individual farmers, the common pastures, and lastly the common forests.[8] The single farm or estate was an independent economic and social unit, and its owner exercised powers that virtually made him a petty king. There were instances where one man owned extensive areas, but small farms cultivated by the owner, the members of his family and perhaps a female slave were also quite common.[9] A farm of twelve cows and oxen and two horses was considered a fair-sized estate.[10] But many parts of the North afforded only limited possibilities for agriculture. Othere said about Norway that " all the land suitable for grazing or cultivation lies by the sea, and is in many places very rock-bound." [11] " While there are large forests in most provinces in Germany," wrote Adam of Bremen, " they are even denser in Jutland, where the people abandon the soil because of its infertility. . . . In some sections there is hardly a spot that is cultivated and inhabitable. But where the fjords cut into the land, large towns are situated." [12]

[7] Knut Gjerset, *A History of the Norwegian People* (New York, 1915), vol. i, p. 111.

[8] *Cf.* Hildebrand, *op. cit.*, p. 178; see also Axel Olrik, *Viking Civilization* (New York, 1930), p. 25.

[9] A runic inscription from Uppland, Sweden, reveals that a certain man, Jarlabanke by name, owned the entire parish of Täby in that province. See Otto von Friesen, *Historiska runinskrifter*, in *Fornvännen, 1909*, p. 83.

[10] Emil Sommarin, *Träldomen i Norden, Verdandi småskrifter no. 104* (Stockholm, 1917), p. 11.

[11] Alfred the Great, *op. cit.* (Bosworth's trans., p. 13).

[12] *Gesta Hammaburgensis ecclesiae pontificum*, iv, 1.

Most of the cleared land was under continual cultivation, and a system of crop rotation was not practiced until after the viking period. The Northmen were aware, however, of the advantages of allowing the land to lie fallow and of using such land for pasture. Stable manure was the only known fertilizer, but the quantities used were insufficient to maintain fertility of the soil.[13] Barley, oats, rye and perhaps some wheat were raised. Other crops included beans, peas, and turnips, and flax and hemp.[14] Grain-growing as such was secondary in importance to cattle-raising, even in Denmark and Southern Sweden, where a higher agricultural development had been reached than elsewhere in the Scandinavian North.[15] Oxen were generally used in the fields, while horses, being more scarce and valuable, were as a rule the property of the wealthy and used for hunting and warfare. The cattle were allowed to roam at will in the forests and the waste lands. In severe winters large numbers starved to death. Throughout the North even the draught horses, where such were found, had to find their sustenance by themselves. The numerous swine remained out in the open the greater part of the time and seem to have fed chiefly on acorns.[16] In the northernmost inhabited part of the Scandinavian peninsula, the farmers brought their cattle to the mountain pastures for the summer months. The vikings learned many things pertaining to agriculture while sojourning in foreign lands, particularly the importance of root crops.[17]

[13] V. Gudmundsson, *"Ackerbau"* in Hoops' *Reallexikon der Germ. Altertumskunde.*

[14] *Ibid.*

[15] See Adam of Bremen, *op. cit.*, iv, 4, 5, 7, 21, 30; *cf.* also A. Bugge, *Norges Historie, Bind* i, *Del* 1, p. 23; and V. Gudmundsson, *loc. cit.*

[16] Gudmundsson and Kålund, in Paul's *Grundriss der Germ. Philologie,* vol. iii, pp. 456-458.

[17] A. Bugge, *Vesterlandenes indflydelse paa nordboernes og særlig nordmændernes ydre kultur, Levesaet, og Samfundsforhold i Vikingetiden* (Oslo, 1905), pp. 254-263.

Iceland and Norway were known for their large herds of sheep. In northern Scandinavia reindeer were kept in large numbers. According to King Alfred's account, Othere had, " when he came to the king, six hundred tame reindeer of his own breeding." [18] Bee culture was also of some importance, especially in Sweden, where the province of Värmland had become famous for its honey.[19]

HUNTING AND FISHING

Hunting or trapping occupied a prominent place in the lives of the Northmen in viking times.[20] Jordanes, who wrote in the sixth century, points to the existence in his day of an extensive export trade in furs which was carried on by the Swedes with Rome.[21] Several centuries later, according to the sagas, there were many people in the North who made a living by " hunting on land and water." [22]

Fishing was always an important source of livelihood in the North. Fresh water fishing was not insignificant, but salt water fishing provided a living for a larger number of people. The Northmen of the viking era went regularly to the fishing banks off shore. Cod fishing was pursued along the entire coast of Norway and gave to the region called Halogaland the economic strength for which it became known in viking times.[23] During the viking period and practically throughout the Middle Ages, herring came in

[18] Alfred the Great, *op. cit.*, p. 12.

[19] K. Weinhold, *Altnordisches Leben* (Berlin, 1856), p. 89.

[20] This is attested to by a wealth of archaeological finds, a number of rock-carvings, as well as statements by the early writers dealing with the Scandinavian North (A. E. Holmberg, *Nordbon under hednatiden*, Stockholm, 1852, pp. 71-73).

[21] *The Gothic History of Jordanes*, 21 (C. H. Mierow's transl., Princeton, 1915, p. 56).

[22] *Egil's Saga*, ch. 4.

[23] A. Bugge, *Norges historie, Bind* i, *Del* 2, p. 28.

large schools to the banks of the coast of Scania.[24]   In viking times large quantities of herring were also caught elsewhere in the North, notably off the coasts of Viken and Jutland. Great schools came to the banks off Halogaland, from which region considerable shipments were made to points further south in Norway.[25]

The fish were cured in various ways, by drying, salting and smoking.   There was very little salt imported to the Scandinavian peninsula prior to the year 1000, and the domestic production appears to have been rather limited, even relatively speaking.   Salt-boiling existed, especially in Norway, and one of the sagas states that King Olav of Norway once prohibited the exportation of " both herring and salt " from Viken to Götaland, a Swedish kingdom, which commodities " the Gauts could ill be without." [26]   Requiring a minimum of salt, the drying process was more prevalent than any other; and the Northmen seem to have known since pre-historic times how to cure the cod by drying it in the open air as well as in open sheds.[27]

The use of nets goes back to pre-historic times and needles for net-making have been found in large numbers in the burial mounds in many parts of Scandinavia.   These burial mounds have also yielded fish-hooks of various sizes.   The gig was known, as was the harpoon, used in whaling by the early inhabitants of the North.   Hook and line were commonly used in cod fishing; and for the catching of other types of fish, the Northmen had numerous other implements.[28]

[24] *Saxo Grammaticus* (J. Olrik's transl., Copenhagen, 1925, p. 188), who wrote in the twelfth century, states that the herring were so plentiful in the Sound by that time that they could be caught with the bare hands.

[25] A. Bugge, *op. cit., Bind* i, *Del* 2, p. 29.

[26] *Heimskringla, Saga of Saint Olav*, 61.

[27] The word " *torsk*," which is the Scandinavian term for cod, meant originally " dried fish " or dried cod (A. Bugge, *Den norske sjøfarts historie*, Oslo, 1923, p. 145).

[28] Gudmundsson and Kålund, *op. cit.*, p. 461.

From King Alfred's account of Othere's trip to the land of the Beormas (Bjarmaland, on the shores of the White Sea) about the year 873, it appears that walruses were caught in Northern Norway in the ninth century.[29] Both the tusks and the hide of the walrus had a commercial value.[30] From the latter, rope was made, which found a wide market not only in the North but also in other parts of Europe.

In foreign lands where they had settled, both in Ireland and in Normandy, the vikings were engaged in whaling. The Arabian writer Quawini, who lived in the thirteenth century and followed the writings of Osmun-Al-Nohuri of the eleventh century, describes whale-fishing along the coast of "*Irlandia*," i. e. Ireland. Bugge believes that these whale-catchers were Northmen and that they brought with them from Scandinavia the practice of hunting whales with the harpoon in the open sea. It is also quite evident, he holds, that they used this method while they still were in Scandinavia, notably Norway.[31] Also in Normandy whaling was carried on by means of the harpoon. Here the whalers worked in groups known by their Old Norse name "*Walmanni*," which means "whale-men" or "whaling-

[29] Alfred the Great, *op. cit.*, pp. 9-12. It is evident that when speaking of the "*hors-whael*" (horse-whale), King Alfred refers to the walrus. "This whale," Othere told King Alfred, "is much less than other whales: it is not longer than seven ells" (Seven ells is the equivalent of fourteen feet). See Bosworth's notes in *op. cit.*, pp. 10-12. *Cf.* also Nansen, *op. cit.*, vol. i, pp. 172 *et seq.* and Japetus Steenstrup, *Dansk Hist. Tidsskrift*, 6 *R.*, 2 *B.*, p. 109.

[30] The British Museum has a set of beautifully carved chess figures of ivory which were found in the Hebrides. They date back to about 1100 and are claimed to have been made by Northmen (A. Bugge, *op. cit.*, vol. i, p. 153). In the same museum there is also the greater part of the well-known Frank's Casket made of ivory which presumably came from the North. King Alfred mentions how Othere and his men brought gifts of ivory to the king and it is quite plausible that the material could have come to England in this way (Nansen, *op. cit.*, vol. i, p. 176).

[31] Bugge, *Norges historie, Bind* i, *Del* 2, p. 29.

men." [32]   Thus both whaling and walrus hunting were pursued in the North throughout the viking period.[33]   Othere speaks of the good whale-fishing in his own country, the coastal region of Finnmarken, where he claims the whales were "eight and forty ells long and the largest fifty ells long." [34]   The Norwegian Gulathings Law (149-150) also contains stipulations pertaining to whaling.[35]   In off-seasons, those participating in fishing and whaling often turned to trade.

[32] Steenstrup, *Normannerne*, vol. i, p. 188.

[33] But toward the close of the eleventh century, whaling began to decline. Peder Clauson Friis, a clergyman of Undal, Norway, stated in his book *Om djur, Fugle oc Traer udi Norge* (1613) that "in the days of old many means and methods were used in catching the whale . . . but because of man's decreasing resourcefulness these methods are no longer used, so that in our day people do not know how to catch the whale except when he drifts ashore to them." See Bugge, *Den norske sjøfarts historie*, vol. i, p. 154.

[34] Alfred the Great, *op. cit.*, p. 11. Further substantiation of the contention that the Northmen, and possibly also the Finns, pursued whaling in this region may be found in the fins of whales that were discovered in a grave on the Haugen farm in Toten in Northern Norway (Bugge, *op. cit.*, vol. i, p. 154).

[35] The Gulathings Law and the Frostathings Law date back, in considerable part, to the eleventh century, or to "the first generation of the Christian Age" (L. M. Larsen, *The Earliest Norwegian Laws*, New York, 1935, p. vii) ; *cf.* the same author, "Witnesses and Oath Helpers," *C. H. Haskins' Anniversary Essays in Medieval History* (Boston, 1929), pp. 134-135. Although "the importance of these codes lies primarily in their detailed presentation of Norwegian life in the two greater centuries of the Middle Ages, they do have an earlier interest leading back into Germanic origins which no scholar can afford to ignore. It is quite true that they belong to a Christian age, but it is also true that the secular laws are not in accord with Christian ethics on every point. Much was added to Norse jurisprudence when the bishops arrived in Norway, but even more was retained. For, Christian or heathen, the dwellers on the North Way continued to live in the old environment, and they kept what they could of the familiar system, since that alone seemed to fit into the circumstances of their social and physical life" (L. M. Larson, *The Earliest Norwegian Laws*, p. viii).

TRADE

The first contacts between the North and the outside world were made thousands of years before the dawn of the viking era. Montelius holds that there were connections between Sweden and England centuries before the birth of Christ. It is also highly probable that the merchants from Greece and Asia Minor who were engaged in the amber trade came to the North as early as the second or third century B. C.[36] The contacts between the Northmen and the Romans came somewhat later.

In the Scandinavian North as well as elsewhere during the Middle Ages, trading involved great risks. There were few roads for vehicles; the forests were dense and extensive and held numerous robbers. As a result the water routes became of greatest significance, but even water transportation was largely confined to the summer months when periods of inclement weather were less frequent and only a minor obstacle. The ships were small and the seafarer seldom ventured far from land. He sailed mostly during the days and anchored in bays and other protected places at night. The merchant or *farman* himself brought his goods to the fair or the market town. Those who owned no ships made arrangements with a *farman* to have their merchandise transported from one market town to another, the merchants themselves going along as supercargoes.[37] On these trips the Northman trader encountered many dangers and difficulties; he was exposed to the attacks of other traders or pirates, and, being a stranger, he had as a rule no legal recourse in the places that he visited. The viking merchant, however, was prepared to cope with these problems. Pirates were met on their own terms and not infrequently subdued.[38]

[36] *Nordisk Tidskrift, 1908,* pp. 302, 383.

[37] Bugge, *op. cit.,* vol. i, p. 134.

[38] See, for instance, Rimbert, *Life of Anskar* (Charles H. Robinson's transl., London, 1921), ch. 5.

In the middle of the ninth century, Danes had settled permanently as merchants in the Frankish kingdom.[39] Danish merchants also resided in a town called Reric, situated on the coast of Mecklenburg.[40] The connections of Reric were chiefly with Saxony and Dorstad, on the Rhine, not far from Utrecht. In time Bruges took the place of Dorstad as the terminal for the Danish trade with Flanders. In 873 a commercial treaty was concluded between Louis the German and the Danish king.[41] The fact that Otto III in 998 exempted the merchants of the " Bishopric of Schleswig " from paying the customary duties in the domains of Germany suggests the existence of commercial relations between the town of Slesvik and Western Germany at that time.[42]

By way of Ripen or Ribe, a town on the west coast of Jutland, went the trade with the West.[43] From Aarhus, says Adam of Bremen, " one sails to Bremen, Funen, Zealand, Scania and Norway." [44] From the Viken district in Norway, merchant ships went to Rouen in France, to the Swedish provinces and to Denmark.[45] Traders from far-

[39] Steenstrup, *op. cit.*, vol. ii, p. 29; W. Vogel, *Die Normannen und das Fränkische Reich bis zur Gründung der Normandie* (Heidelberg, 1906), p. 46.

[40] A. Bugge, *Vierteljahrsschrift für Sozial- und Wirtschaftsgeschichte*, iv, 1906, p. 237. From Reric the Danish king Godfred is said to have collected considerable amounts in custom duties. *Cf.* Steenstrup, *Venderne og de danske før Valdemar den Stores Tid* (Copenhagen, 1910).

[41] A. Bugge, " *Handel* " in Hoops' *Reallexikon der Germ. Altertumskunde; Annales Fuldenses*, 873.

[42] Hasse, *Schleswig-Holstein-Lauenburg, Regesten und Urkunden*, vol. i, n. 31. Quoted from Bugge, *loc. cit.*

[43] *Life of Anskar*, ch. 32.

[44] *Gesta Hammaburgensis* ..., iv, 1.

[45] *Heimskringla, Saga of Saint Olav*, 146, 61.

away places in turn visited Viken.[46] In Western Norway, the ecclesiastical center of Nidaros had also become a trading mart of some consequence, and it appears to have been the definite aim of King Olav Tryggvason, the founder of Nidaros, to make the city the center of the trade of Northern Norway.[47] Through Nidaros went the trade between Iceland and the rest of the world.

Iceland, colonized chiefly by Norwegians in the last quarter of the ninth century, had close commercial ties with the mother country. Although no ships were built in Iceland, the Icelanders also participated in the trade of the North during the viking period.[48] A certain Thorold is mentioned

---

[46] "The men of Viken knew Christian customs better than the folk in the North of the land, because there were in the Vik both in winter and summer many merchants, both Danes and Saxers. The men of the Vik also went much on trading journeys to England, and Saxony, Flanders and Denmark, and some went on viking raids and had winter settlements in Christian lands" (*ibid.*, 64).

[47] A. Bugge, Hoops' *Reallexikon, loc. cit.*

[48] Lumber was virtually non-existent in Iceland. This contention has been unsuccessfully opposed by a number of writers. The rigid climate of Iceland does not permit trees to grow sufficiently large so that lumber may be obtained from the logs; and there is nothing to indicate that the climate of Iceland was more favorable to vegetation a thousand years ago than it is today. There is an old German poem "*Merigarto,*" probably from the latter half of the eleventh century, which contains some enlightening lines on this question:

> "When I came to Utrecht, I found a good man,
> . . . . . .
> A pious priest, of perfect goodness.
> He told me truly, as many more there [also said],
> He had sailed to Iceland . . . there he found much wealth . . .
> With meal and with wine and with alder-wood.
> This they buy for fires, for wood is dear with them.
> . . . . . .
> There a bundle of alder-wood is given [sold] for a penny."

(Müllenhoff and Scherer, *Denkmäler dtsch. Poesie und Prosa,* Berlin, 1892. vol. ii, p. 196). The English version is from Nansen, *op. cit.*, vol. i, p. 181. *Cf.* also K. Gjerset, *A History of Iceland* (London, 1924), pp. 77-78, and A. Bugge, *Den norske trælasthandels historie* (Skien, 1925), vol. i, p. 61.

as a great merchant who owned a trading vessel with which he went on voyages to many places, among them Dublin.[49]

Trade in the North in viking times was inextricably bound up with piracy and robbery on land.[50] Upon entering a foreign port, the viking ships hoisted a red shield, indicating a peaceful mission.[51] The seafarers then proposed peace with the townsmen for a certain number of days or weeks. During these periods of peace no plunder was permitted, and arrangements would be made for a fair. Then, when the period of peace had expired, the vikings would depart for other fields to engage in pillage or trade, as conditions permitted. At times they returned to pillage the very town where they had been trading only a short time before. Thus it is said about the two brothers Egil and Thorolf Skall-agrimsson that they went to Courland, " first trading but when that was ended, they took to harrying, now here and now there." [52] In the *Heimskringla* we read that when Tore the Hound and Karli " came to Bjarmaland, they lay in to the market town, where there was at that time a market and the men who had money with them all got wares in plenty. Tore got many fur, beaver and sable; Karli had also much goods with which he bought many skins. And

---

[49] *Eyerbyggjasaga*, 29.

[50] " Piracy was the initiative of maritime trade among the Greeks of the Homeric era, as among the Norse vikings; for a long time the two vocations developed concert" (H. Pirenne, *Medieval Cities*, Princeton, 1925, p. 109).

[51] This was another function of the shield, in addition to the one of being a protective armor. A raised shield meant that the bearer came on a friendly mission. A shield hoisted on a city gate, as, for instance, when Oleg hoisted a shield on the gate of Constantinople, was " a sign of victory" (*The Russian Primary Chron.*). See also Steenstrup, *Norman-nerne*, vol. i, pp. 360-361, and Karl Lehman, *Kauffriede und Friedenschild, Germanistische Abhandlungen zum 70. Geburtstag Konrad von Maurers* (Göttingen, 1893), p. 60.

[52] *Egil's Saga*, ch. 48.

when the market was at at end, they sailed out along the River Vina (N. Dvina), and the peace with the men of the land was then ended." When they were at sea again, Tore asked the men if they " were eager enough to go on land and win goods for themselves." As the answer was in the affirmative, a profitable raid was made.[53]

A tendency toward a " division of labor " is first discernible in the latter part of the viking period. By this time the Northmen engaged in foreign enterprise may in a general way be divided into two groups, one comprising primarily merchants and another consisting of those who made plundering their chief occupation. The lines of demarcation, however, were not very rigid. " Björn was a great man in sea-faring, who sometimes went a-viking and sometimes on trading voyages," states the *Egil's Saga*.[54]

The merchant vikings assembled at certain times of the year at definite ports, whence they sailed as one fleet to some distant trading town.[55] But the purpose of these fleets was not entirely to strengthen the defense and to provide greater security against other merchant-pirates. It was equally desirable to enhance the offensive power of the merchants; for if they perchance should meet an inferior fleet, they might be in a position to appropriate some of the ships and the cargoes, including the men for the slave-trade.

As was the case in other parts of Europe, there emerged also in the North a number of fairs which played an important rôle in the commerce of the Middle Ages. In times these fairs came to coincide with the pagan celebrations, as at Upsala, and later with the Church holidays. The result

[53] *Saga of Saint Olav*, 133.

[54] Ch. 32.

[55] One of the best known of these convoys was the " Sound fleet " (*Eyrasund floti* or *Eyra floti*) which received its name from the fact that it was formed in the Sound.

was that several ecclesiastical centers, notably Nidaros or Trondheim, became trading marts of considerable importance.[56]

A number of trading towns flourished in the North in viking times. Some of these were fortified and had a permanent population while others were unfortified and of no account except when the fairs were in progress.[57] But they were all commercial centers and generally owed their existence to a superior geographical location near some highway of trade. Of these towns or cities Birka, Hedeby-Slesvik and Skiringssal were the most important. Others were Halör (Halye) in the Sound and Brännö and Konungahella on the River Göta in Sweden.[58]

Birka, situated on the island of Björkö in Lake Mälaren in Sweden, was not only one of the earliest cities of the North, but also the first town in which the population lived chiefly upon the returns from shipping and trade.[59] The city appears to have been planned as a trading center, which suggests that the first settlers were not warrior vikings but primarily merchants. Judging from what is told in connection with the visit of Anskar to the North, Birka was of no importance prior to 800, but reached its height in the ninth century. The city was destroyed sometime after 970; the latest coins found on Björkö were stamped in that year.[60]

[56] The name of Visby, the famous trading center on Gotland, is derived from *vé*, an old word meaning sanctuary. Odense in Denmark was originally called *Othens-vé*, i. e., Odin's temple or sanctuary (Sophus Bugge, *Studier over de norske byers selvstyre og handel for Hanseaternes tid*, Oslo, 1899, p. 5).

[57] A. Schück, *Fornvännen, 1924*, p. 17.

[58] "Halye is the place in all the North to which the greatest crowds come when there is a market there" (*Saga of Faroe Islanders*, 2).

[59] A. Bugge, *Vierteljahrsschrift für Sozial- und Wirtschaftsgeschichte*, iv, p. 234.

[60] Wadstein, *Norden och Väst-Europa i gammal tid* (Stockholm, 1925), p. 89. Sture Bolin (*Scandia*, vol. iv, 1933, pp. 244-250) is of the opinion

The favorable location of the town of Hedeby—or Slesvik (Schleswig)—made it the center of the transit trade between the Baltic and the West.[61] The ships went as far as Hollingstadt, from which point the goods were transported overland to Slesvik and from there the remaining short distance to the North Sea. Rimbert speaks of Slesvik as a place where people from many parts of Europe came to transact their business.[62] Especially lively was the intercourse with Dorstad and Hamburg, and fleets of merchant ships sailed at regular intervals from Slesvik to Birka in Sweden. Adam of Bremen, who speaks of the commercial importance of Slesvik in the eleventh century, states that the city at that time was populous and wealthy. " In its harbor ships from Slavonia, Sweden, Semland and even Russia and Greece may be seen." [63] The population of Slesvik was chiefly Frisian, but the town played an important rôle as a place where marauder vikings exchanged their booty for precious metals or other commodities.

Skiringssal, the oldest trading center in Norway, was located a few miles to the northeast of the present day Larvik. The town disappeared about 900 and was succeeded by Tunsberg, now Tonsberg.

that the city fell during the latter part of the eleventh century. The sacking was presumably done by vikings who had heard of its wealth. According to Adam of Bremen (*Descr. Ins. Aquil.*, ch. 48), Birka had several times been attacked by vikings.

[61] This town is mentioned by Einhard (*Annales, 804, 808*). Early references to Slesvik indicate that the town at one time had been called " Sliesthorp ", i. e., the " Dorf on the Schlei." In the Icelandic sagas Slesvik is the term applied to the innermost bay of the Schlei; the Danes called the town Hedeby (Old Norse *Heidabýr* or " the city desert "). In time the name of Hedeby was lost, while that of Slesvik or Schleswig survived.

[62] *Life of Anskar*, chs. 24, 33.

[63] *Gesta Hammaburgensis*, iv, 1.

The most important commercial region of the North was the island of Gotland in the Baltic Sea.[64] Because of its advantageous geographical location, Gotland had become a trading center as early as the time of the Great Migrations, and its importance increased markedly during the viking age.[65] The commerce between Russia and Western Europe went largely through the towns of Gotland, of which Visby was the foremost.[66] The presence of an abundant supply of precious metal in Gotland constituted a strong incentive on the part of other Northmen to attack its towns. A runic inscription from Torsätra in Uppland, Sweden, reads as follows: "Skule and Folke raised this stone in memory of their brother Husbjörn. In foreign lands he increased his wealth and exacted tribute also in Gotland." [67] Gotland belonged to Svealand in a personal union under her king and paid a yearly tribute to him.[68]

The sagas refer to organized exploitation of the Laplanders by way of trade. In the Baltic these exploiters were called "Birkarlar," i. e., "Men of Birka." Their Norwegian counterpart were the participants in the "Finnkaup," i. e., the trading with and the collecting of taxes from the

[64] Bugge, *Den norske sjøfarts historie*, vol. i, pp. 65-66.

[65] The *Guta Saga* (4), written down in the middle of the thirteenth century but based on older accounts, states that "although the people of Gotland were heathens, they sent their ships everywhere and carried on trade with both Christians and heathens."

[66] The older Visby, inhabited by Gutes, apparently lost its power about 1100. The Visby of Hanseatic fame came into existence as a result of a marked influx of German merchants in the twelfth century and seems to have been somewhat different in character from the Visby of the viking and pre-viking era. *Cf.* A. Schück, *Fornvännen, 1924*, p. 17.

[67] Erik Brate and Sophus Bugge, "*Runverser*," in *Antikvarisk tidskrift för Sverige*, vol. x (1887-1891), p. 66.

[68] *Cf.* however, B. Nerman, *En utvandring från Gotland och öns införlivande med Sveaväldet, Kungliga Vitterhets, Historie och Antikvitetets Akademien, Handlingar, Del 34* (Stockholm, 1929), p. 70.

Laplanders.   This trade was a royal monopoly which prior to the last quarter of the ninth century appears to have been held by the kings of Halogaland.[69]   The tax, consisting of furs, feathers and tusks and skins of the walrus, was paid according to the wealth of the tribesmen.[70]

A rather typical example of the trade in the North in viking times is referred to in connection with one Thorolf Kveldulfsson who in the year 900 sent a " great-ship built for the main sea " to England laden with " dried fish and hides and white-ware [white furs]," as well as other furs. The crew " set sail home again in the Autumn " with a return cargo of " wheat and honey, wine and clothes." [71] Honey gained its importance as a commodity in trade from the fact that it was the sugar of those days and was needed for the making of mead, the standard drink of the Northmen.[72]   Most of the malt, another ingredient for mead-brewing, apparently was produced in Denmark; one of the Norwegian kings is said to have sent some of his men " south to Denmark to buy heavy things: malt, wheat and honey."   Grain was also imported from Frisia and Northern Germany.[73]

[69] See *Egil's Saga*, chs. 10 and 13.

[70] " ... the richest must pay fifteen skins of the marten, and five of the reindeer, and one bear's skin, and forty bushels of feathers, and a bear or otter-skin kirtle, and two ship-ropes, each sixty ells long, one made from the whale's hide, and the other from the seal's " (Alfred the Great, *op. cit.*, p. 12).

[71] *Egil's Saga*, ch. 17; see A. Bugge, *op. cit.*, vol. i, p. 161.

[72] Wine gained in favor with the Northmen during viking times; in fact, it was largely because of their desire for wine that they undertook some of their expeditions to western France.   Steenstrup, *op. cit.*, vol. i, p. 185; see *infra*, p. 133.   As a rule, the wine which was brought to the northern countries as a commodity in commerce did not come from the wine-producing districts directly, but was secured in England and Frisia.

[73] Bugge, *op. cit.*, vol. i, p. 161.

The slave trade was of considerable importance in viking times. Harald Fairhair is said to have paid off his men with " women slaves from the East." [74] The slave business constituted a prominent part of the viking activities along the Volga and in Constantinople.[75] Northmen slave traders were also active in Bristol and other centers in the West. The foremost slave market in the North itself seems to have been Brännö in Sweden.[76]

Mention is also made of an export trade in hunting hawks from Norway, which was the king's monopoly. The archbishops of Nidaros also bought up " geir-hawks, gray hawks and pigeon hawks," but the king's permission was necessary to enter the business. In the eleventh century, during the reign of William the Conqueror, the town of Worcester in England was obliged to pay a tribute to the king of " ten pounds or a Norwegian hawk." In the twelfth and thirteenth centuries both Englishmen and Norwegians came to Iceland to procure hawks for their respective countries.[77]

Prior to the viking period, and to an extent also during that period, trade was mostly barter, but payments in gold and silver occurred. These metals were generally made into bars, rods and rings from which pieces were cut and weighed. The weighing of the precious metals was continued even after the introduction of coins, because of the

---

[74] *Fagrskinna*, ch. 6.

[75] See " *Ibn Fadlan's Account of Scandinavian Merchants on the Volga in 922,*" in *Journal of Engl. and Germ. Philology*, vol. xxii (1923).

[76] Here an Icelander at one time bought a female slave who later turned out to be an Irish princess. Her exceptional beauty induced the Icelander to pay three marks for her, although the prevailing price of a female slave was only one mark (*Laxdaela Saga*, ch. 12). The price of slaves varied of course like that of any other commodity; the ordinary price of a male slave seems to have been three marks, while a female slave fetched one mark or the same as a good cow or ox (E. Sommarin, *op. cit.*, p. 22).

[77] Bugge, *op. cit.*, vol. i, p. 158.

irregular sizes of the latter as well as the prevailing practice of clipping. Silver was the unit of value in the viking age, and the coins in circulation, both those of the North and the more numerous ones of non-Scandinavian origin, were silver coins. The oldest provincial law code of Sweden states that in the early Middle Ages one *öre* in gold had a value of one " mark weighed silver." Since one mark was the equivalent of eight *öre,* the proportion was 8 : 1. Silver was, consequently, a great deal more valuable in those days than in more recent times.[78]

Close to 40,000 Arabic coins have been found in the Scandinavian North, some in such remote places as Lapland and Iceland. The great majority of them, approximately 24,000 whole and 14,000 fragmentary Arabic coins, have been found within the Swedish domains. Many of these coins originated in Kufu, a city near the Euphrates, while others came from Central Asia. The Historical Museum of Oslo holds several coins of this type, which, having only a thin silver coating, are counterfeit. A considerable part of the coins from the East belongs to the pre-viking era. Both in extent and completeness, the collection of Anglo-Saxon coins in Stockholm rivals that of the British Museum.[79] Approximately 25,000 coins from the viking period have been found in Sweden alone during the last century and a quarter, and numerous stories from the past suggest that many more were found during the eighteenth century which were not preserved but melted down. Montelius has stated that the many finds in the Swedish soil constitute probably only a fraction of one per cent of the total that was buried in it.[80] The largest discoveries have been made in the vic-

[78] Montelius, *Sveriges förbindelser med andra länder i förhistorisk tid,* p. 7.

[79] See W. Cunningham, *Growth of English Industry and Commerce* (Cambridge, 1922), vol. i, p. 89.

[80] *Sveriges förbindelser med andra länder,* p. 4.

inity of Lake Mälaren, and especially on Öland and Gotland, regions chiefly of commercial import. Since the great majority of the marauder vikings active in England came from Denmark, the west coast of Sweden, and from Norway, it is likely that the coins were not buried immediately upon having been secured in England, but were used for some time in commerce.[81]

The basic sources of livelihood in the North were agriculture, fishing, hunting and trade. Of considerable influence in the growth of the viking movement were also the social and legal institutions to which we now turn.

[81] Montelius, *Forntiden*, in *Sveriges historia intill tjugonde seklet* (E. Hildebrand, ed., Stockholm, 1903), p. 245; H. Shetelig, *Det norske folks historie* (Oslo, 1930), vol. i, p. 251.

CHAPTER III

SOCIAL ORDER

THE prevailing social order in the North was decidedly aristocratic in nature. Birth and wealth determined the social stratification which found expression in a number of ways. In the banquet halls, for instance, there were " high-seats " and " low-seats; " the most humble sat by the door. In the continental parts of the Scandinavian North, it was not easy for an individual to climb from one rung of the social ladder to another. In Iceland, on the other hand, under conditions that a new country afforded, a more fluid society made shifts from one class to another easier and more common.

Foremost in this aristocratic order was the " high-born " class, from which the rulers of the respective nations or kingdoms were chosen. To this class belonged also the jarls, who generally were local chieftains or petty kings ruling over neighborhoods or smaller regions. The name jarl indicated, on the whole, an office rather than a hereditary title. In Norway, the jarls were holders of grants of land, bestowed upon them by King Harald Fairhair toward the close of the ninth century, after he had unified the country. Their duty was to raise a certain number of soldiers in case of war, to support the king and his following when they were traveling through the country, to enforce the laws and to collect taxes, one third of which they retained.[1] In Denmark and Sweden royal families had ex-

[1] Ebbe Hertzberg, *En fremstilling af det norske aristokratis historie indtil kong Sverres tid* (Oslo, 1869), p. 16. The most unpopular tax of those imposed by Harald was the " nose-tax," a personal tax levied on every household according to its number of " noses."

isted in the various regions or smaller "kingdoms" long before the viking period began.[2] Some of these families had lost their power when the larger kingdoms, notably those of Götaland and Svealand in Sweden, had been formed. The power and prestige of virtually all of them were further impaired during the era of viking aggression.

The king was elected by the landed classes to rule for an indefinite period; if the other high-born men or the nobles were dissatisfied with his rule, he was summarily deposed and another was chosen in his place. In Svealand, for example, the king was elected by the free men of the land assembled at Mora Rocks, near Uppsala. The king represented the unity of the country, but his other functions were not clearly defined. His authority sprang chiefly from exigencies of war, as the Northmen realized that centralized authority was essential to success in combat. Adam of Bremen writes about the Swedes that they " have kings of an old line whose powers depend upon the opinions of the people at large [nobles and other land owners]. The king must accept what the people jointly have decided, unless his opinion seems better, in which case they follow him. Therefore they proudly proclaim that at home they are all alike. In war they render the king, or the man whom the king has placed at the head, complete and unquestioned obedience."[3] Although wealthy, powerful and the first citizen of the land, the king was never looked upon as one who could do no wrong.[4] "If the king attacks a man in his house," says the Norwegian *Frostathings Law* "[men shall]

[2] Henrik Schück believes that there were no jarls in Svealand in viking times; in Götaland and other parts of Sweden, they were to be found, however (*Svenska folkets historia*, Stockholm, 1914, vol. i, p. 325).

[3] *Gesta Hammaburgensis* . . . , iv, 22.

[4] L. M. Larson, *op. cit.*, p. 21.

go upon him and slay him, and if he escapes, he shall never be allowed to return to the land." [5]

Next in order came the nobles, who during the earlier period were patriarchal chieftains called " *hersar.*" The founders of this class had originally been military men or chosen leaders of armies who on retiring had been invested with certain administrative and judiciary duties.[6] In a sense they were the king's liegemen, but real feudalism never existed in Scandinavia proper; only in Denmark do we find evidences of it.[7] Iceland, whence came many participants in the enterprises abroad during the latter half of the viking period, remained for some time " a group of chieftaincies without any tie of union under a central government." A large number of the *landnámsmenn* (i. e., settlers) had been important men in Norway, who retained their social standing also in Iceland.[8]

The third class comprised the bonder (singular bonde), the great landed middle class, ranging from the petty freeholder, who possessed only a conditional title to his land, to the owner of " odal land," i. e., land recognized as belonging to a certain family. At the beginning of the viking period, the bonder were an independent, well-to-do class. As the viking era progressed, however, the status of the bonder changed greatly. As a class, the noblemen seem to have gained more from marauding overseas than the odalmen, who heretofore had constituted the dominating group among the bonder. Similarly, many individual freeholders became successful viking leaders abroad and upon their return to the North were able to secure more land, the pre-

[5] *Frostathings Law*, iv, 50.

[6] E. Hertzberg, *op. cit.*, p. 17.

[7] See Paul Vinogradoff, *Cambridge Medieval History*, vol. iii (1913), p. 652.

[8] Knut Gjerset, *op. cit.*, p. 30.

vailing token of prestige, from other freeholders. Thus, though some *hauldar,* i. e., owners of odal land, gained considerable fame and wealth in foreign lands, the bonder as a class, and the odalmen in particular, lost ground. They were reduced the most in Denmark, but retained more of their independence farther North, especially in Sweden.[9]

Last among the non-servile Northmen were the freedmen, who comprised ex-slaves and a number of generations of their descendants. They were free, semi-skilled laborers who worked for a compensation, partly paid in kind. Among them were also individuals, or descendants of individuals, who had dropped from a higher station in life to the rank of the cottier.[10]

Slavery had existed in the North since pre-historic times. The early slave population had been augmented by Celtic and Slavic captives brought to the North after successful campaigns in foreign lands. Only exceptionally did the Northmen enslave their own kind, as in payment of a debt or as a punishment for a crime.[11] Some individuals who were unable to support or protect themselves, voluntarily surrendered their freedom. In Sweden such slaves became known as " gift-slaves " (*gävträlar*). The slaves performed most of the heavy work on the farms. Thus it was the duty of the woman-slave " to tend the gristmill and milk the cows," as revealed by the Swedish provincial law code of the Westgoths.[12] For damages caused by slaves, the slave-

[9] E. Hertzberg, *op. cit.,* p. 9; M. W. Williams, *Social Scandinavia in the Viking Age* (New York, 1920), p. 48.

[10] E. Hertzberg, *op. cit.,* p. 17.

[11] E. Sommarin, *op. cit.,* p. 20.

[12] The various provincial law codes of Sweden took form in the twelfth and thirteenth centuries, but depict, nevertheless, " a social order that in many respects was the same as that of the viking age " (H. Schück, *op. cit.,* vol. i, p. 159).

owner was held fully liable.[18]   Although slaves were found
in the North as late as the thirteenth century, manumission
had begun centuries earlier.   Erling, a great landowner in
Norway, " set his thralls to do daywork and gave them time
afterwards, and allowed every man to work for himself at
dusk or in the night.   He gave them acres to sow corn
thereon for themselves and produce crops for gain.   He
set a price and ransom on every one of them, and many freed
themselves the first year or the second; all who were thrifty
enough had freed themselves in three years.   With his
money Erling bought himself other thralls.   Some of his
men he turned to herring fishing and some to other trades.
Some cleared woods and built themselves farms there." [14]

Throughout the North most of the estates remained in
the hands of the land-owning families from generation to
generation, and during the greater part of the viking period
they were, as a rule, not bought and sold, but transferred to
new owners only as an inheritance or in conjunction with
marriage between members of different families.   In many
parts only male descendants could inherit the land, but
women had, in certain places and under certain conditions,
a lawful right to " both odal and movables." [15]

[18] The liability for damages caused by slaves appears to have been
greater than that for the depredations made by cattle. "If cattle damages cattle, horn or hoof or thrall, it shall be paid at half value" (*The
Bjarkö-Ret*, 140, in *Norges Gamle Love indtil 1387*, ed. by R. Keyser and
P. A. Munch, Oslo, 1846, p. 329).

[14] *Heimskringla, Saga of Saint Olav*, 23. For other references to the
manumission of slaves, see the *Gulathings Law*, 61, and the *Frostathings
Law*, ix, 12. The clearing of land came to be looked upon as being below
the dignity of the free man. We read in one of the sagas that a certain
Olav went into the region which later became known as the province
of Värmland in Sweden in order to clear land and to make room for
settlers. "But when they heard in Sweden about Olav, how he was
clearing the land, they called him Tree-feller [or wood-carver] and his
position seemed to them disgraceful" (*Heimskringla, Ynglingasaga*, 42).

[15] See *Gulathings Law*, 275. There is an interesting saga account from

If the owner of odal land wanted to sell his holdings, the kinsmen had the first option; they had the " allodial right," as it still is called in Norway.[16] This right could be exercised over a long period of time at the instant the owner took steps to dispose of his land by sale.[17] The conception that the land belonged primarily to the family (*ätt*) prevailed also in Sweden. The *Gutalag* states that " if those nearest of kin are unable to buy the land that someone is compelled to sell, then their rights shall pass to more distant relatives, for land must not be sold outside of the family." [18]

Iceland which suggests that it was also possible to acquire property through " holmgang," if properly arranged and executed. (Holmgang was a duel fought on a holm or a small island in a river or lake.) Thus we read that a certain Ljot, because of his actions, " was little sorrowed after by most men." Having " no kinsfolk there in the land, he had come thither and gathered himself fee by holmgang." The holmgang law at this time, the saga asserts, stipulated that if the challenger was victorious, he was to receive the object for which he had challenged his opponent. If the challenger lost, he should pay the fee previously agreed upon, " but if he fell on the holm, then he forfeited all his possessions " and the victor " should take heritage after him." Being eager to profit by this law, Ljot is said to have challenged his neighbors for their estates or have provoked them to the extent that they had challenged him. " He had felled many good bonders, and in this manner had become greatly wealthy both in lands and loose goods " (*Egil's Saga*, ch. 64).

[16] The *Gulathings Law* (270) classifies " the various kinds of odal land " as follows: " 1. Land that has been passed from man to man for five successive generations; 2. Land that has been acquired in payment of wergild; 3. Land received as foster inheritance; 4. Land received as gift or mark of honor; 5. Land received from the king as a gift for hospitality; 6. Land received as foster payment; 7. Land received in exchange for odal land. . . . All other land is money land." Larson's transl., p. 178. A. Taranger holds that " the real odal-land was the arable land, the tilled ground, the ' fenced in' fields, meadows and pastures, in fact the homestead," and not all the land belonging to an odal-man (Paul Vinogradoff, ed., *Essays in Legal History*, Oxford, 1913, p. 160). As to the kinsmen's option, the *Gulathings Law* (276) states: " . . . the man's son has the first right to buy."

[17] " Twenty winters " or " before three kings have passed away." See *Gulathings Law*, 271-272.

[18] C. J. Schlyter, *Samling af Sweriges gamla lagar*, vol. vii.

The Northmen were long very reluctant to divide their estates.   One son, generally the oldest, received the homestead, while the other sons inherited arms, ships and " the sea." [19]   But with the lapse of time new conditions set in. As a result of the viking enterprises money became more plentiful in the North, and some of the old estates were purchased by returning marauders.   Regretting the passing of " the good old days " and lamenting the mercenary spirit of his age, a saga-teller of the latter part of the viking period states that " even ancestral homes are now being sold for money." [20]

The many stipulations relative to hunting found in the old provincial law code of Västergötland show that the hunting rights went with the ownership of the land.   The purpose of many of these rules was to prevent ruthless depletion of animal life and to aid its perpetuation, in order to safeguard a supplementary food-supply as well as the income derived from the fur trade.   There were periods during which the killing of certain game was penalized by a fine, but the effective collection of this fine seems to have been problematic.   The squirrel and the hare were the animals thus protected.   It was unlawful to kill them during the period from March to October when " they do not carry their winter furs."   The old provincial law codes also mention wolf-yards, wolf-ditches and wolf-nets.   These contrivances were made and maintained as common enterprises, and any farmer who failed to contribute his share paid a fine.   The laws of the later Middle Ages which made it compulsory for every able-bodied man to participate in a posse, should one be called for, grew out of a necessity for col-

[19] On the question of primogeniture, see, however, Steenstrup, op. cit., vol. i, p. 251.

[20] Heimskringla, Saga of Saint Olav, 67.

lective action against the wolf and the bear in viking times, or long before these laws were put in writing.[21]

The old provincial law codes of Sweden as well as the Norwegian *Gulathings Law* suggest that the right to fresh-water fishing rested with the owners of land along the lakes and rivers or with those to whom this right had been conveyed in the course of time.[22] This pertains particularly to the salmon fishing, which was, and still is, the most important fresh-water fishing in Scandinavia. Deep-sea fishing was free to all.

Among the fishermen were not only men from the lower classes but occasionally also members of the upper stratum of society. Thus the son of Ingemund, a prominent Icelander, took part in the fishing " because it was customary in those days that the children of prominent folk also did work of some kind." But by the general run of the people, fishing was pursued in order to procure food. Some possessed their own boats, while others worked on boats that partially or entirely belonged to someone else. It is said about Thorolf, one of the Icelandic saga-heroes, that he " swept much into his own net of those takings that there were in Halogaland: had men of his in the herring-fisheries and so too in the cod-fisheries." [23] In certain regions, especially on the rockbound and generally infertile islands and shoreline along the coast of Northern Norway as well as in Iceland, fish appears literally to have been man's " daily bread." One year, it is told, when the soil and the sea had been extremely niggardly, a school of herring finally appeared. It was then Eyvind the Skald, for want of food

[21] A. E. Holmberg, *op. cit.*, p. 73.

[22] " No one shall go to fish in another man's stream; if he does he fishes for the benefit of him who owns the stream; and he shall pay the fine for trespass to the owner of the stream " (*Gulathings Law*, 85).

[23] *Egil's Saga*, ch. 11.

was compelled to exchange his arrows—his last possessions —for a few herrings.[24]

From bitter experiences of crop-failures and famines the people of the North had become accustomed to store up grain for the lean years.[25] It was the duty on the part of the possessors of such " old grain " (Old Norse *forn korn*) to share it with those whose crops had failed.[26] The problem of securing grain for seeding purposes was especially difficult in the lean years. The small land owner was often compelled to use all his grain for bread or for feed for his cattle, so that when sowing time came, nothing was left for seed. Such a person, however, could request that the bailiff or king's representative in his district appoint a committee comprising capable and impartial individuals to ascertain if there were surplus grain on other farms. By surplus grain was meant quantities not needed for the owner's household prior to the time that a new crop could be expected, or for the planting of his own land. If, in the committee's judgment, surplus grain was found on a farm and the owner

[24] *Heimskringla, Saga of Hakon Jarl,* 13.

[25] The Asa-religion demanded sacrifice to Odin in years of famine. The *Ynglinga Saga* states that in King Domaldr's days "there was famine and need in Sweden. The Swedes then held a great sacrifice near Uppsala. For the first harvest they sacrificed oxen, but the crop was not bettered by it; for the next harvest they sacrificed men, but the crop was the same or even worse. For the third harvest many Swedes came to Upsala; the chiefs took counsel and held to a man that Domaldr must be the cause and that they should have to sacrifice him in order to have a good season, that they should bear their weapons against him and dye the altar with his blood. And so they did." Likewise, when Olav Trätälja in Värmland gave few blood offerings, " the Swedes liked that ill and thought that bad seasons came through it. They gathered an army, went against King Olav, surrounded his house and burned him in it; they gave him to Odin and made blood offerings in order to have a good season" (*Heimskringla, Ynglinga Saga,* 15, 43).

[26] Referring to hay, the *Saga of Hen Thorir,* ch. v, states " .... for it is meet that they should sell who have."

refused to part with it, the king's representative had the power to seize it and distribute it among those who lacked seed. The recipients were to return an equivalent quantity as soon as they had harvested their crops in the following fall.[27]

As has already been indicated, the North was divided into a number of politico-military units. This was particularly true in Sweden and Norway, where many dense forests and not easily traversed mountains constituted effective barriers between the various regions. Each one of these units or provinces possessed a distinct group solidarity. This is suggested by the Swedish law codes of Västergötland and Västmanland, where people from other provinces are referred to as " foreigners." This group solidarity is also noticeable in the overseas campaigns. In the armies of the Northmen a highly developed sense of solidarity toward one's own unit, although not necessarily with regard to other viking forces, is found. Just as there was a superstitious belief in the North that luck would fail the crew of any fishing boat as soon as dissension occurred among the men, so they believed that luck would never remain with any army that allowed dissension to creep in.[28] That there was nothing pan-Scandinavian in this solidarity is suggested by the conflict between the Seine vikings and the Somme vikings in the Carolingian Empire in 861, and the bloody battle of Carlingford Loch in 851 between the Danes and the Norwegians over the supremacy in the Irish field.[29]

There are records from Iceland which indicate that the language constituted a tie of considerable significance in

[27] Gudmundsson and Kålund, *op. cit.*, p. 460.

[28] " It was the talk at that time that fishermen's luck would fail them if they fell out among themselves, and most of the men so believed and were careful" (*Laxdaela Saga*, ch. 14). See also Gudmundsson and Kålund, *op. cit.*, p. 460.

[29] See *infra*, p. 116.

their national consciousness.   It is stated in one of the Icelandic law codes that if a " foreign man " from the three
lands where " our tongue " is spoken, i. e., Denmark,
Norway and Sweden, is killed in Iceland, the relatives shall
have the same right of prosecution as the Icelanders themselves; but foreigners from the lands where our tongue is
not spoken, cannot prosecute except in the case of father,
son and brother, and then only if the murdered man was
known in Iceland.[30]   In the North at large, however, legal
jurisdiction overshadowed the ties of language and religion.
The *things* or court sessions were the real centers of the
Northmen's communal existence.   The importance of legal
jurisdiction is suggested by the graduated rate of the wergild,[31] as stipulated by the law codes of the Westgoths and
the Gotlanders which date back to the century following the
viking period.   The former states that the amount of the
wergild for the murder of a native of the province or kingdom of the Westgoths (Västergötland) should be twenty-
one marks; for a native of Svealand, slightly more than
thirteen marks; for a Dane or Norwegian, nine marks; and
for a German or an Englishman, four marks.[32]   The law
code of the Gotlanders stipulated twenty-four marks for a
Gotlander and ten marks for others.[33]   The outlawing of
Ganger-Rolf, a great viking, high-born and a favorite of
King Harald Fairhair, appears to have been the result of a

[30] *Grágás*, iii, 171; Williams, op. cit., p. 33.

[31] The wergild was a fine paid by the kindred of the slayer to those
of the slain.

[32] H. S. Collin and C. J. Schlyter, *Samling af Sweriges gamla lagar,*
vol. i; Nat. Beckman, *Äldre Västgötalagen, översatt och förklarad*
(Upsala, 1924), pp. 17-18.   For a detailed account of fines and their distribution in south-western Norway, see *The Gulathings Law*, 222-252 and
316-319.   These stipulations " show clearly what an appalling business the
practice of exacting wergild had come to be" (L. M. Larson, *op. cit.*, p. 15).

[33] C. J. Schlyter, *Samling af Sweriges gamla lagar*, vol. vii.

confusion on Rolf's part as to the existing jurisdictional boundaries of Norway. One autumn while on his way home from a viking expedition to the West, Rolf found his provisions depleted upon reaching the coast of Norway. In the accepted viking manner, he permitted his men to go ashore and fetch what they thought they needed. But in doing so, he either forgot or was unaware of the fact that King Harald had previously gone into this region with his army, and that the people had acknowledged him as their king. Incensed over Ganger-Rolf's depredations, the people complained to the king, and we find that neither Rolf's high birth nor the intercession of his mother could save him. At the next thing Ganger-Rolf was convicted of deliberate piracy and outlawed.[34] Had Ganger-Rolf been harrying in the same region before its population had pledged itself to King Harald Fairhair, there would have been no case against him.[35]

No one could count on safety of life and property while outside his immediate kingdom. At home the individual had the aid of his kin, friends and neighbors in combating invading strangers. Raids in regions under a different legal jurisdiction did not constitute violations of any laws. The mere fact that there were " costly halls and fertile fields " to be found in neighboring kingdoms was considered a legitimate reason for an attack.[36] Likewise, an outsider had every right to seize whatever he could; and the Northman knew that only physical inability, laziness or indifference would prevent the " foreigners " from taking his possessions. A state of war existed as a matter of course, and the very calling of the viking stood for marauding and warfare in regions that were under a different legal jurisdiction.

[34] *Heimskringla, Saga of Harald Fairhair*, 24.
[35] Emil Svensén, *Striden för freden* (Stockholm, 1910), p. 15.
[36] *The Poetic Edda, Lay of Rig*, 49.

In the measure that the coups in foreign lands became increasingly profitable, the occupation of marauding gained in prestige at home. When a high-born young man announced that his father had furnished him ships and that he was selecting men for an expedition, the young men of the country-side vied with one another for a place on his ships. As late as the year 1000, Olav, Norway's future saint and national hero, called together the young men of his acquaintance and went plundering on foreign shores. The runic inscription over many a warrior states that " in foreign lands he sought gold and booty " or " gold and honor." In the Edda much prominence is given to treasures of precious metals hidden in the ground. Mimer, the god of wisdom and inspiration, is also the " Treasure-Mimer," or the guardian of the riches of the world.

The gods were never on the side of the one who refused to engage in battle. The Norns, or the shield-maidens of Odin, wove the web of victory and defeat.

The web is woven of the guts of men and weighed down with human heads. There are blood-stained darts to form the shafts; its stays are iron wrought, with arrows shuttled. Strike with your swords this web of victory.

Now the web is woven and the field reddened. Bloody clouds are gathering over the sky. The air shall be dyed with the blood of men. Let us ride very fast on our bare-backed steeds, with our drawn swords in our hands, far away.[37]

" I saw how the Northmen had arrived with their wares, and pitched their camp beside the Volga," relates Ibn Fadlan, an Arabian traveler. Every one carries an axe, a dagger, and a sword, and without these they are never seen. . . . When a son is born to one of them, he flings down a

---

[37] *Corpus Poeticum Boreale* (ed. by G. Vigfusson and F. York Powell, Oxford, 1883), vol. i, p. 282. " Bare-backed steeds " meant ships.

sword saying, ' Only that is yours which you win with your sword.' " [38]

" Tell me this," said Hakon Jarl to Sigmund, " in what do you put your trust? " Promptly Sigmund answered, " I put my trust in my strength and good right arm." [39] A conspicuous example of a viking leader is Egil Skallagrimsson of Burg in Iceland. As a child Egil was moody and " masterful and angry tempered." When seven years old he killed an older boy who had beaten him in a ball game. This escapade convinced his mother that there was " viking-stuff " in her son, and she counselled that they buy him warships as soon as he was old enough to command them. Once, when Egil was twelve years old, he was about to be chastised by Skallagrim, his father. But Thorgerd Brak, a woman of Skallagrim's household who had fostered Egil in his childhood, interfered. Incensed over her temerity, the father struck at Thorgerd, who fled and leaped off a cliff into the sound. " Skallagrim cast after her with a great stone, and sat it between her shoulders, and neither it nor she came up again." The death of Thorgerd angered Egil, and that same evening when Skallagrim and his men sat down to eat, Egil walked up to his father's steward, " who was most dear to Skallagrim," and resolutely cut him down. " But Skallagrim spake naught of this, and that matter lay quiet henceforth between them." [40]

---

[38] *Ibn Fadlan's Account* . . . , p. 56. Ibn Fadlan also adds: " Never did I see people so gigantic; they are tall as palm trees, and florid and ruddy of complexion. . . . The women carry, fastened to their breast, a little case of iron, copper, silver, or gold, according to the wealth and resources of their husbands. Fastened to the case they wear a ring, and upon that a dagger, all attached to their breast. About their necks they wear gold and silver chains. If the husband possesses ten thousand dirhems, he has one chain made for his wife; if twenty thousand, two; and for every ten thousand, one is added. Hence it often happens that a Scandinavian woman has a large number of chains about her neck" (*ibid.*).

[39] *Saga of the Faroe Islanders*, 22.

[40] *Egil's Saga*, ch. 40.

Under the prevailing type of justice, considerable significance was attached to the brotherhood, consisting of both natural and " sworn " brothers. " Bare is the back of the brotherless," says an old Scandinavian proverb. The " sworn brotherhood " (Old Norse *fostbrœdra-lag*) was entered into by two young men who wished to make their friendship more binding.[41] The selection of the " sworn brothers " was by no means random. In addition to the congeniality of temperament of the two young men, the wealth, good will and fighting strength of the respective families that they represented were the determining factors. Especially numerous were the " sworn brotherhoods " among the participants in the viking enterprises abroad.

The prevailing form of society fostered also conditions under which blood feuds flourished. These blood feuds often had a direct bearing upon the undertaking of the viking enterprises, since many a viking was a slayer who judiciously had left the country in order to avoid being killed, or an outlaw for whose exploits no wergild had been paid. The blood feuds continued long after a more orderly society had been established, but gradually the system of paying wergild was adopted. It was assumed that a man represented a definite value and that his family should be compensated for the loss that his death entailed. At first the disparity in strength that the killing of a man brought about was counteracted by causing a similar loss in the ranks of the kindred of the first offender. Later the loss was calculated in monetary terms and took the form of the wergild.

[41] The ceremony included their gashing themselves and permitting the blood to mingle in fresh soil uncovered by the cutting of the sod. Kneeling on the ground, the two men thereupon would beseech all the gods to bear witness of their agreement, each swearing to avenge any wrong done the other, just as they would have done had they been natural brothers. A handclasp sealed the pact (*Gisla Saga Surssonar*, 13-14; M. W. Williams, *op. cit.*, p. 25).

The amount of the wergild was not uniform. We have seen that it varied as to the remoteness of the domicile of the victim. Likewise, the fine imposed upon an outsider was higher than the one demanded from a fellow townsman or a resident of the same legal district.[42] There were also variations as to the social class of both victim and offender.[43] The Swedish *Björköa-rätten* (XII, 2) contains the stipulation that " murder which occurs on the public square before noon shall be fined by 80 marks, after noon by 40 marks." [44]

In Denmark and Sweden the laws stipulated that the whole kindred of the slayer must contribute to the payment, and that the wergild should be divided among the kindred of the slain, even if they were not his direct heirs.[45] The payment to be made by each member of the kindred varied with his relationship to the murderer, according to a graduated scale, those of the first line of kinship paying the most; those of the second line, half the amount of those of the first; and so on down the line. Thus, since the payment was fixed, the amount to be paid by each individual varied with the size of the family, and the amount received by each kin

[42] A similar distinction was also found in England between the conquerors and the conquered. A reading of the " North People's Law " ... " suggests that the Danes estimated their own wergilds at twice the value of the Angles, just as in early days the Saxons had valued themselves at twice as much as the wealh" or Briton (Stubbs, *The Constitutional History of England*, Cambridge, 1897, vol. i, p. 199).

[43] R. Keyser, *Efterladte skrifter*, vol. ii (Oslo, 1867), p. 303; Steenstrup, *op. cit.*, vol. iv, p. 290; *cf.* M. W. Williams, *op. cit.*, p. 311.

[44] C. J. Schlyter, *op. cit.*, vol. vi.

[45] B. Phillpotts, *Kindred and Clan in the Middle Ages and After* (Cambridge, 1913), pp. 68-101) ; M. W. Williams, *op. cit.*, p. 29. The Swedish provincial law code of the Westgoths awarded six marks to the direct heirs and six marks to the *ätt* or kindred. Practically throughout Sweden the wergild was divided into three equal parts ; one part went to the district or county (*härad*), one to the king, and one to the heirs, including both direct heirs and members of the kindred. See Steenstrup, *op. cit.*, vol. iv, p. 290.

of the slain naturally varied in a similar manner.[46] The early Scandinavian law codes also contain elaborate stipulations for pecuniary compensation for wounds and the loss of limbs.[47]

The provincial law code of Scania (V, 12) states that the indemnity for a person's eye, hand or foot was half of that for his life. If both eyes, hands or feet were destroyed, full *mansbot* or wergild was due.[48]

A monetary value was also given to an individual's " personal rights." [49] In the Gula province in Norway the " rights " of a high-born man were valued at six marks. A *hauld* or bonde could claim three marks and a common freeman one and one-half marks. A freed-man whose emancipation had been duly published had a right to six oras.[50] Although variations existed in the different regions, these rates appear to have been typical for the North as a whole. From this treatment of the institutional setting, we turn to a consideration of the numerical strength of the Northmen in viking times.

[46] *Gulathings Law*, 222.

[47] *Ibid.*, 185, 215; *Frostathings Law*, 12, 42-49, 53, 57, 60.

[48] Schlyter, *op. cit.*, vol. ix; *cf.* Steenstrup, *op. cit.*, vol. iv, p. 306.

[49] By " personal rights " were meant " the rights that every one enjoyed as members of the social body, particularly the right to be compensated for wrongs and injuries to oneself or to one's kindred. To be deprived of 'right' was equivalent to exile" (Larson, *The Earliest Norwegian Laws*, p. 426). See *Gulathings Law*, 200. Measures were taken to prevent abuses of the law. " No one, either man or woman, has a right to claim atonement more than three times, unless he has taken revenge in the meantime" (*Gulathings Law*, 186).

[50] Larson, *op. cit.*, p. 14.

CHAPTER IV

POPULATION

EVERY estimate of the population of the North in viking times must necessarily be very indefinite in nature. Johannes C. H. R. Steenstrup, the foremost student of the viking movement, sought to obtain some information on this point by making an investigation of the chronicles and the annals of the ravaged regions, with regard to the number of ships engaged in the various attacks and the number of people slain.[1] The records suggest that there was on the whole a marked increase in the number of ships in the viking fleets as time went on. The first expeditions seem to have been undertaken in comparatively small fleets, consisting of any number from two or three to about forty ships. On the basis of Steenstrup's estimate of no less than forty men per ship, the early fleets seem to have carried only fair-sized contingents.[2] But by 880 the viking armies appear to have become quite large. Several thousand men are said to have fallen in the battle of Saucourt.[3] Thousands of warrior vikings also took part in the siege of Paris in 885, and the army under Rollo in 911 was also very large.

The chronicles which depict conditions in the latter half of the tenth century are even more emphatic than the earlier

[1] *Op. cit.*, vol. i, pp. 210-217.

[2] Even in Russia where river navigation necessitated the use of smaller ships "forty men [were] reckoned to a ship" (*The Russian Primary Chron.*, 907). It is true that Einhard (*Annales, 812*) claims that 10,940 men were left fallen after the battle between Sigfrid and Ring, the two pretenders to the throne of Denmark, but this is doubtless an exaggeration.

[3] Various numbers have been given; the *Annales Fuldenses* state 9,000.

ones in their stress upon the large numbers of participants in the viking raids.   The writers are astonished by the rapidity with which reenforcements arrive from the Scandinavian North, and the attacks are described as a continual devastating storm from the North.   The Northmen are said to have been " as numerous as grasshoppers and to have covered the whole earth."   Large waves of foreigners, the Irish annals relate, rolled from the sea up over Erin.   " The sea spewed out fleet upon fleet, and no harbor or anchor place, no fort or skaw was without a fleet of ships." [4]

About a century ago, H. M. Velschow estimated that the population of Denmark in the early part of the tenth century was about 550,000.   Velschow further estimated that in the middle of the thirteenth century the population was approximately 1,550,000, with a possible error of from twelve to fifteen per cent.   With boundaries as of 1885, Velschow's estimate would give an approximate figure of 958,000 for the year 1250. [5]   The latter estimate was rejected by Kr. Erslev, who arrived at a much lower figure, or approximately 340,000 for the same time and region. [6]   Steenstrup points to Velschow's conclusions that Jutland, for example, had the same rural population in 1250 that it had in 1840—or about 748,000—and infers that the population three centuries earlier very likely was about the same.   Even if the cultivation of the land was less intensive during the vik-

---

[4] *War of the Gaedhil with the Gaill, or the Invasion of Ireland by the Danes and other Norsemen* (J. H. Todd's ed.), pp. 10-20, 41.

[5] *Dansk Hist. Tidsskrift, 1 Række, 4 Bind* (1843), pp. 1-52.   Velschow built his estimate on the information given in the *Knytlinga Saga* (ch. 32) that Denmark was divided into 850 ships' districts (*skipæn*).   The regional distribution of these districts is given as follows: Skåne, then a part of Denmark, had 150, Zealand 120, Fyn 100, Borglum *stift* 50. Viborg 100, Aarhus 90, Ribe 110 and Slesvig 130.   Each district was divided into sub-districts (*havne*) each of which in turn comprised a certain number of farms or estates.

[6] *Dansk Hist. Tidsskrift, 5 R., 5 B.* (1885), p. 519.

ing era than in later times, it is possible, Steenstrup believed, that the forests, the sea and the lakes could have contained more food than in more recent years.[7] Both the archaeological finds and the sagas indicate considerable dependence upon fishing and hunting for the necessities of life, but foodstuffs were also imported, particularly from England and Frisia.[8]

In Sweden, Hans Hildebrand sought to ascertain the size of the population of that country in the Middle Ages on the basis of the Peter's Pence, the tax paid to the Pope by the various bishoprics of Sweden. Hildebrand concluded that in the first half of the fourteenth century, the earliest period to which these receipts lend themselves, there were nearly 520,000 people in Sweden.[9] What the population was four or five centuries earlier must necessarily remain a matter of great conjecture. It has been estimated, however, that the population of the entire Sweden in viking times was slightly more than 500,000, while that of the island of Gotland was about 60,000 or approximately the same as the present-day figure.[10]

The population of Norway in the tenth century was "somewhere between two and three hundred thousand."[11] Iceland had in all likelihood forty or forty-five thousand in 930 and perhaps close to sixty thousand in 965.[12]

[7] Steenstrup, *op. cit.*, vol. i, p. 218.

[8] See *supra*, p. 32.

[9] Between 1333 and 1350, the tax receipts suggest the following average population in the various bishoprics: Uppsala, 104,640; Linköping, 132,480; Skara, 77,760; Strängnäs, 129,020; Västerås, 65,380; Växjö, 13,440. The total is 522,720 persons. But it is to be noticed that Scania, Bleking and parts of Småland were not included (H. Hildebrand, *Sveriges medeltid*, Stockholm, 1879, vol. i, p. 59). See also Montelius, *Svensk Tidskrift*, 1890, pp. 201-203.

[10] J. Nihlĕn, *Under rutat segel, svenska äventyr i Öster* (Stockholm, 1928), pp. 39-40.

[11] H. Hermannsson, *Islandica* (Ithaca, 1930), vol. xx, p. 64; *cf.* James Bryce, *Studies in History and Jurisprudence* (Oxford, 1901), vol. i, p. 266.

[12] *Safn til sogu Islands*, iv, pp. 357-384; Hermannsson, *op. cit.*, p. 6.

There are saga references which suggest an actual over-population in the inhabited areas of the North. It is said about the province of Värmland in Sweden that " the hard times were caused by the fact that there were more people in the land than it could hold, and so the inhabitants went out and conquered Solör." [13] That the pressure of population long remained a serious problem in the North is further suggested by the fact that the Northmen tenaciously held to the practice of exposing children, even after Christianity had taken a rather firm hold and was able to influence human conduct in other respects.[14]

The records also suggest that the Northmen were a highly sensual people. Their exploits in England and the Carolingian Empire show that they possessed to a marked degree the sexual brutality of most invading hordes and armies.[15] Even more revealing is the report of the Arabian emissary Ibn Fadlan, who encountered the viking merchants on the Volga about 922. He states that upon reaching the market town, the Northmen constructed booths or houses in which they transacted their business. " Each man has a couch, where he sits with the beautiful girls he has for sale. Here he is as likely as not to enjoy one of them while a friend looks on. At times several of them will be thus engaged, each in full view of the others." [16] Ibn Fadlan's account

[13] *Heimskringla, Ynglinga Saga,* 43. The saga points out that " the Swedes were wont to give the king the blame both for good and bad years." But " the wisest men of Sweden found out that hard times were due to the folk being more numerous than the land could support, and the king was not to blame for it."

[14] Steenstrup, *op. cit.,* vol. i, p. 221.

[15] " Very often they [the Northmen] seize the wives and daughters of our thanes, and cruelly violate them before the great chieftains' faces " (*Lupi Sermo ad Anglos, Res. Dan.,* vol. i, p. 469).

[16] *Ibn Fadlan's Account,* ..., p. 55. The reactions of the cultured Arabian traders and travelers of that day, who also included Ibn Dustash and Masudi, to the manners and customs of the " wild and war-loving

also shows that sex orgies constituted a prominent part of their funeral rites.[17] Another illustration may be taken from

Northmen" are far from flattering. This, in the words of Montelius, "was not the fault of the writers." See Montelius, *Sveriges förbind. med andra länder, . . . ,* p. 4.

[17] One of their chieftains died, and, following their custom, his family asked his girls who was to die with him. The one who volunteered was "committed to two girls, who were to keep watch over her wherever she went." While the dead man was being prepared for burial, " the girl gave herself over to drinking and singing, and was cheerful and gay."

The chief's ship had been drawn up on land and surrounded by piles of wood. They "brought a couch, placed it on the ship and covered it with Greek cloth of gold, wadded and quilted with pillows of the same material. There came an old crone, whom they call the angel of death, and spread the articles mentioned on the couch. . . . It was she who was to slay the girl." The dead man was carried "into the tent and placed in the ship," and "strong drink, fruits, and basil" were placed beside him. "Then they brought a dog, which they cut in two, and threw into the ship; laid all his weapons beside him; and led up two horses which they chased until they were dripping with sweat, whereupon they cut them in pieces with their swords, and threw the flesh into the ship." Two oxen, a cock, and a hen were likewise killed and thrown into the ship.

"The girl who had devoted herself to death meanwhile walked to and fro, entering one after another of the tents which they had there. The occupant of each tent lay with her, saying, 'Tell your master, "I [the man] did this only for the love of you."'

Having been lifted into the ship, the girl was given several cups of strong drink. Then "the hag seized her by the head and dragged her into the tent. At this moment the men began to beat upon their shields with the staves, in order to drown the noise of her outcries which might have terrified the other girls, and deterred them from seeking death with their masters in the future. Then six men followed into the tent and each and every one had carnal companionship with her." Thereupon the girl was placed at her master's side. The old woman "knotted a rope around her neck, and handed the ends to two of the men to pull. Then with a broad-bladed dagger she smote her between the ribs, and drew the blade forth, while the men strangled her with the rope until she died."

"The next of kin to the dead man, followed by others, then put fire to the ship. "Before an hour had passed, ship, wood and girl had, with the man, turned to ashes."

Speaking to one of Ibn Fadlan's countrymen, one of the Northmen said, "You Arabs must be a stupid set! You take him who is to you the

a saga account that describes an incident at the fair of Brännö, near the present-day Gothenburg. When " strolling about bent on diversion," Höskuld (an Icelander) " came upon a large and handsome tent " owned by Gille, a wealthy merchant. Höskuld was shown three women whom he looked over very carefully. He bought one of them " who to him seemed very fair," and " that same night went to bed with her." [18] The wealthy and more prominent men of the day had a number of wives, as well as concubines. Harald Fairhair, for instance, is said to have dismissed nine earlier wives when he married Ragnhild.[19] In Iceland every man could have two wives, one at home and one in Norway; the children of both were considered legitimate.[20] Adam of Bremen says about the Swedes that there was no limit to the number of wives a man might take. " Each one has according to his wealth, two, three or more, but the rich and foremost among them have innumerable ones, and the children of all are considered legitimate.[21] In Normandy, where the Northmen had accepted Christianity, many of them continued to take wives " *danico more*," i. e., to take another wife in addition to the one married in the Christian fashion.[22]

Whether there was a connection between this marked sensuality of the Northmen and the surplus of man-power in the North in viking times is not readily ascertained. Steen-

---

most revered and beloved of men, and cast him into the ground, to be devoured by creeping things and worms. We, on the other hand, burn him in a twinkling, so that he instantly enters Paradise." . . . Having said this, " he burst out into uncontrolable laughter" (*Ibn Fadlan's Account*, . . . , pp. 59-60).

[18] *Laxdaela Saga*, ch. 12.

[19] *Heimskringla, Saga of Harald Fairhair*, 21.

[20] *Gragas*, iv.

[21] *Gesta Hammaburgensis*, . . . , iv, 21.

[22] Steenstrup, *Normandiets historie* (Copenhagen, 1925), ch. 13.

strup, who believed that the Danish expeditions were due to over-population in Denmark, found the causes of the latter in extreme sensuality, polygamy and concubinage.[23]   There are statements in the sagas to the effect that the vikings at times brought back concubines from foreign lands; and this practice may have contributed, in a measure at least, to a high birth rate.

The non-Scandinavian sources, such as the annals and the chronicles, state that the Northmen armies were very formidable and suggest, thereby, that there was an abundance of man-power in the North in viking times.   It is possible, of course, that future studies will show that many of the figures pertaining to the size of the invading Northmen forces, handed down to us by the annalists and chroniclers, have been greatly exaggerated.   We have seen that, on the basis of the estimates of the Scandinavian historians, the total population in the North in viking times was probably a little more than one million people, and very likely less than a million and a half.   The inhabited and cultivated areas were confined to the coast lines and the lake and river valleys inland.[24]   Furthermore, as has been pointed out in an earlier chapter, the agricultural skill of the vikings was not very great.[25]   Considerable quantities of sustenance were obtained from the outside.[26]   These imports were paid

[23] Steenstrup, *Normannerne*, vol. i, pp. 222-242.

[24] H. Schück, *op. cit.*, vol. i, p. 184.

[25] See also V. Gudmundsson, *"Ackerbau"* in Hoops' *Reallexikon der Germ. Altertumskunde.*

[26] See *Egil's Saga*, ch. 17, and *Heimskringla, Saga of Harald Fairhair*, 36.   Such importations continued even after the viking period.   At a *thing* in Bergen about 1186, King Sverre of Norway said: "We thank all English men who bring hither wheat and honey, flour and cloth, for coming; we thank also all men who bring hither linen, wax or kettles. We will also name those who have come from the Orkneys, Hjaltland (Shetland), Faroes, Iceland and all those who bring into this land things useful for it" (*Formmanna Sögur*, vii; Bugge, *Den norske sjøforts historie*, vol. i, p. 174).

for with precious metal which was plentiful in the North at this time.[27] Most of the wealth came to the North as returns from the exploitation of other peoples. During the pre-viking and early viking period, the inhabitants of the East Baltic region and Russia were the chief victims. Later, the area which the Northmen were able to tap was greatly extended, chiefly to the West. Thus, in spite of the " niggardly nature " of the North itself, it seems that prevailing conditions enabled a relatively large population to emerge and exist.

The abundant supply of man-power obviously contributed to the success of the viking enterprises oversea. Of even greater significance was the high development reached by the Northmen with regard to the technics of aggression, evidenced by their superior ships and forms of organization.

[27] S. Bolin, "*Vikingatåg*" in *Nordisk Familjebok*; H. Hildebrand, "*De öster- och västerländska mynten i Sveriges jord*," in *Festskrift tillägnad C. G. Malmström* (Stockholm, 1897), pp. 9 *et seq.*; *cf.* B. Nerman, *Studier över Svärges hedna litteratur* (Upsala, 1913), pp. 20-21.

CHAPTER V

Ships, Organization and Tactics

At the time of Tacitus the art of shipbuilding in the North was still on a rather primitive level, judging from his statement that the fleets of the *Suiones,* i. e., the Swedes, consisted of row-boats without sails. The testimony of Tacitus is substantiated by the Nydam find.[1] There is nothing to indicate that sails were used in the North prior to the eighth century,[2] but by this time the ships of the Northmen were superior to those of other peoples. In England, as well as on the Continent, the ships were crude and clumsy, unsuited for open-sea sailing. In Ireland, despite the fact that the inhabitants were an island people, seafaring to any appreciable extent did not exist. Here the coracle, which precluded the undertaking of extensive voyages, was still used.[3] The viking ships, on the other hand, were larger than the average craft of the times and much easier to navigate. "In the beauty of their form, and the perfection of their design (given the material, technique and general plan)," the sea-horses of the North "surpassed all other craft that ever set wings to wood."[4] They enabled the

---

[1] The Nydam boat, from the third or fourth century, was found in 1863 in the Nydam Bog in Schleswig. Built of heavy boards of oak, it is 70 feet long and 11 feet amidships. It shows no signs of having been equipped with a sail. See Nansen, *op. cit.,* vol. i, p. 244.

[2] *Cf.* however, *ibid.,* p. 245.

[3] W. Vogel, "*Nordische Seefahrten im früheren Mittelalter,*" in *Meereskunde,* vol. i, pt. 7, pp. 12-14. The coracle is a small fishing boat made of hides stretched over a wicker frame.

[4] S. C. Gilfillan, *Inventing the Ship* (Chicago, 1935), p. 46.

Northmen to move from place to place with unprecedented dispatch, and many of them were sufficiently well built to withstand the strain that open-sea sailing entailed. This quality of speed and easy maneuvering, making possible a quick descent upon some foreign shore and an equally quick departure, contributed in no small measure to the success of many a viking undertaking. In the development of their technique of shipbuilding, the Northmen had borrowed from the peoples of the Mediterranean world. Striking similarities are noticeable between the ships of the Baltic and those of the Mediterranean, similarities which can hardly be ascribed to two independent developments. Even the old Scandinavian term *dreki,* used to denote the larger viking ship the prow of which was decorated with a head of a dragon or some animal, may have been derived from the Greek δράκων.[5]

The great majority of the ships of the warrior vikings were built for the transportation of troops, and not for encounters on the high seas. In the Anglo-Saxon Chronicle for the year 851 we read that " this year came 350 ships to the mouth of the Thames and the crew landed and took Canterbury and London by storm." In 893, according to the same source, " the great army . . . came again . . . with 250 ships. Then soon after that Hasten with 80 ships landed at the mouth of the Thames." Under the year 849, the *Scotorum* chronicle states that " a naval expedition of seven score ships of the people of the king of the Foreigners came to oppress the Foreigners who were in Erinn before

---

[5] See Vogel, *op. cit.,* p. 25. How the influences from the South were brought to the North is not easily ascertained. The conclusions arrived at by Montelius (*Sveriges förbindelser med andra länder,...*), with regard to the contacts between the North and the regions to the South of the Alps, indicate that overland or river routes played a much more significant role than the sea-routes around the coast of Western Europe. *Cf.* Nansen, *op. cit.,* vol. i, p. 244.

them." Toward the close of the viking period the North-men began to build ships specifically for sea-battles, and the more important naval battles mentioned in the literature were fought between rival fleets of Northmen. During the greater part of the viking period there were no real fleets elsewhere in Europe with which the Northmen could engage in battle, except the fleets of the Moors in Spain and of King Alfred, both of which succeeded for a time in checking the viking onslaught.[6] Realizing that without large and powerful ships a successful stand against the vikings would be impossible, King Alfred had ships built that measured up to sixty pairs of oars.[7] At first a number of these new ships foundered and were lost because of inept handling, but soon the English acquired considerable skill in seamanship and naval strategy; and the traditional " strike and leave " method of attack became less profitable on the shores of England. In 897 nine of Alfred's new ships managed to trap six Danish ships as they lay at anchor in a small bay near the Isle of Wight. Three of the Danish ships tried to fight their way through; one succeeded while the other two were captured and their crews killed. Later the remaining three viking ships took advantage of the tide and slipped away. But two of them ran ashore not far from there and the men were all captured and hanged. There seems to be

---

[6] Thus, in 859, according to Ibn-Adhari, the Northmen found the shores of Spain well guarded, as " the ships of the Moslems cruised in the sea from the boundary of France in the East to the coast of Galicia in the farthermost West." In this attack of 859, the Moors captured two ships that had become separated from the main fleet of the Northmen, and again, in the following year, two viking ships were captured and two more were burned (*Anglo-Saxon Chron.*). In the summer of 875, King Alfred fought against seven enemy ships and captured one of them. In 882, King Alfred fought against four Danish ships, two of which were taken and the men on board killed. In 885, King Alfred sent a fleet to the coast of East Anglia where it captured sixteen viking ships (*ibid.*).

[7] *Anglo-Saxon Chron.*, 897.

only one recorded victory of the Northmen in a battle at sea against non-Scandinavian opponents. That was in 885, on the very same day that the fleet of King Alfred had defeated sixteen viking ships off East Anglia. On their way home, the Anglo-Saxons met a large Danish fleet, and " the Danes won the victory." [8]

In the beginning of the viking period relatively few types of ships were used, but in the course of time new models were being constructed to comply with the requirements of an expanding and more highly specialized business. For piracy and the transportation of the expeditionary forces the " long ships " were most common. There were several variants of this type of craft which differed from each other as to size and design. The size of the vessel was indicated in terms of the number of pairs of oars that it had; a ship that was equipped with twenty row-benches was termed a " twenty-seater," one having thirty row-benches was called a " thirty-seater " and so on. The most common " long ship " measured twenty pairs of oars and was capable of carrying, including the forty oarsmen, perhaps as many as one hundred men. Ships measuring twenty-five or more pairs of oars were called " great ships." In this class belonged the " dragon ship " and the " *skeid*," which was the ship of the wealthier vikings. In addition there were smaller " long ships," such as the " *snekkja*," as well as several other types of smaller craft.[9] The " *knörr* " was primarily a merchant vessel, but was also used for the transportation of troops and occasionally for actual conflict.[10] Being relatively high and broad in proportion to her length, the " *knörr* " was better able to negotiate a rough sea than the longer and narrower " long ship " or " dragon ship; " for

[8] See Steenstrup, *op. cit.*, vol. i, pp. 266-269.

[9] Vogel, *op. cit.*, pp. 35-36.

[10] At the battle of Hafrsfjord, for example, in 872.

this reason she was generally used for longer voyages, such as the expeditions to Ireland, Greenland and North America. Professor W. Hovgaard, the naval authority, states that the seagoing capacity of vessels of this type " was hardly inferior to that of later sailing-vessels of much larger size. Their great beam, their flat bottom, and their extremely light construction made them follow the wave slope without any accumulation of rolling. They would rise readily to the waves and be little liable to ship great quantities of water under ordinary conditions of wind and sea." [11] The " *knörr* " had fewer row-benches than the " long ship " and relied therefore chiefly upon her sail and the wind for power. The row-benches were placed near the prow and the stern so that the space amidships could be utilized for cargo. With the exception of the two half-decks on which the row-benches were fixed, the entire hull of the average merchant ship constituted one large hold over which a sail was suspended to keep out spray and rain.[12] The " *knörr* " could accommodate about fifty men and had a displacement of fifty tons and upward.[13]

It has already been stated that the average " long-ship " was a " twenty-seater," but there were of course also those which measured considerably more. The flagship of King Olav Tryggvason, the " Long Serpent," is said to have had thirty-four row-benches and to have measured some 160 feet over-all. For a time this ship, which carried 250 or more warriors, was the largest in the North, but before long even larger ones were being built. When Cnut set out to conquer England, he is said to have had ships measuring sixty pairs of oars. The best example in existence of a viking " long-

[11] *The Voyages of the Norsemen to North America* (New York, 1914), p. 58.

[12] Hjalmar Falk, *Kulturhistorische Zeitschrift*, vol. iv (1912), p. 48.

[13] Vogel, *op. cit.*, p. 28.

ship " is the Gökstad ship from the eighth century.[14]   This
ship had an over-all length of slightly more than one hundred feet and a displacement of about thirty tons.   She was
equipped with a mast that could be raised and lowered and
with a large square sail.   In addition she had sixteen pairs
of oars which were worked through circular oar-posts.   Her
prow and stern rose boldly from the water line.   The outside of her gunwales was lined with large circular shields,
alternately black and white in color.   The rudder was fixed
over the starboard quarter.   She had five portable berths
forward and a striped tent amidships for the purpose of
providing shelter when not at sea.   While her crew must
have numbered about forty men, she could carry close to
seventy men.[15]

The " monoxyla " (μονόξυλα) were boats built in Russia [16]
especially for the Russian rivers, which often made it necessary for the Northmen to carry their crafts considerable
distances overland past the rapids or from one river to
another.[17]   The Greek writers said they were nothing more

[14] *Ibid.*, p. 23.   The state of the art of shipbuilding in the North in
viking times is best illustrated by the Oseberg ship.   This vessel, Queen
Asa's yacht and subsequent burial ship, was clearly never used in the
pursuance of the viking enterprises, but designed specifically for pleasure-
cruising in the Norwegian fjords.   She had an over-all length of close
to sixty-five feet and was fifteen feet wide amidships.   In addition to
mast and sail, she was equipped with fifteen pairs of oars to be applied
when occasion arose.   Restored, her graceful lines and beautiful carvings
are truly remarkable.

[15] N. Nicolaysen, *The Viking-Ship from Gökstad* (Oslo, 1882), pp.
62 *et seq.*

[16] The Slavs were compelled by the Northmen to cut timber in the
forests and to float the logs down to Kiev in which town the latter had
established shipyards (Const. Porphyrogenetus, *De Administrando Imperio*,
Bonn, 1840, ch. 9).

[17] " *Nordmanni desperatis rebus naves per terram cum magno sudore
trahunt.*", Pertz, *Scriptores*, vol. i, p. 601.

than dug-out canoes.[18]   But even in Russia, fair-sized ships were at times in use.   The ships which Oleg sent against the Greeks in 907 are reputed to have carried forty men each;[19] and Constantine Porphyrogenetus speaks of twenty " pamphyles " which together carried 830 men.[20]

The smaller ships of the earlier period of viking aggression were open boats, while the general run of those of the later period were either partly or fully decked.   Most of them were of oak and built in the clinker-fashion; that is, when the ship was finished, each board would slightly overlap the one just below it, from the gunwale down.   Rivets or bolts of wood, bronze or iron were used, and the seams and joints were caulked with pitch, generally mixed with wool or cow's hair.   One tier of oars was most common. The oars were long and generally worked through holes along the gunwale.   In the smaller crafts the oarsmen sat upon planks extended across the ship, but the larger vessels had individual benches which also seem to have served as chests or lockers for the keeping of the personal belongings of the oarsmen.[21]   The oar-shaped rudder was fixed at the right side of the vessel, looking from stern to bow; consequently, this side of the ship came to be called the " steerboard " (Old Norse *stjórnbordi*), while the opposite side, which was at the back of the helmsman, was called " backboard " (Old Norse *bakbordi*).

The viking ships had as a rule only one mast, which could be raised and lowered, and one sail.   The sail was generally made of heavy woolen cloth (Old Norse *vadmal*), with

---

[18] Some of the boats were apparently so small that men could carry them on their shoulders ... (Const. Porphyrogenetus, *op. cit.*, ch. 9).

[19] *Russian Primary Chron.*, 907.

[20] *De Cerimona*, ii, 44.

[21] V. Gudmundsson, *Nordboernes Skibe i Vikinge- og Sagatiden* (Copenhagen, 1900), p. 19; Hj. Falk, *op. cit.*, p. 73.

stripes or squares of different colors.[22]   Below deck, space
was provided for food and drink.   Some of the ships were
also equipped with small cabins, but as a rule the men remained on deck throughout the voyage, sleeping in sacks
of skin.

Coast sailing predominated, especially during the earlier
part of the viking period.   When a storm approached, the
seafarers sought the shores for protection; even in fair
weather they would cast anchor for the night in some placid
bay along the coast, and frequent trips ashore would be
made in order to procure food and drink, as only a minimum
of provisions was carried along on board the ship.   Under
such conditions the meals were generally prepared ashore.
The members of the crew seemingly took turns at preparing
the meals, and no one in particular was designated to serve
as cook.   When open-sea sailing was necessary, sufficient
quantities of provisions for the voyage were carried along,
and the meals were prepared on board the ship.   In crossing
larger bodies of water, the Northmen were guided by the
sun and the stars.   The Polar Star especially was their guide
and came to be called the "guiding star" (Old Norse
leidarstjarna).[23]

Even according to present-day standards for commercial
craft under sail, the ships of the Northmen were capable of
making a fair speed.   Othere relates that he sailed from
Halogaland, in northern Norway, to Skiringssal, in the
southern part of the country—approximately 950 nautical
miles—in one month.   Allowing for the usual anchoring at
night and a sailing day of twelve hours, this indicates a

[22] "One day when Åsmund was rowing through a sound, a byrding
(i. e., ship of burden) sailed towards them; it was easily recognized, for
it was painted on the bows with white and red; the sail was striped"
(*Heimskringla, Saga of St. Olav*, 132).

[23] Vogel, *op. cit.*, p. 35.

speed of slightly less than three knots. Adam of Bremen says that with a fair wind one could sail from Denmark to England in three days and nights, indicating a speed of five nautical miles per sailing-hour. In the " *Landnámabók* " we read that in fair weather " seven half-days " were needed for a trip from Cape Stadt in Norway to the east-coast of Iceland, a distance of about 570 nautical miles. This suggests a speed of somewhat less than seven knots. But Vogel believes that such a rate was rather uncommon; it is more likely, he contends, that from two to four knots were made by ordinary coast-sailing vessels, from four to six knots when the wind was favorable, and that only occasionally were eight or nine knots ever attained.[24]

The art of shipbuilding reached a higher level in the North in the viking times than anywhere else in Europe. " The builders of such ships were artists," says S. C. Gilfillan, referring to the Gökstad ship.[25] When King Olav Tryggvason had his " Long Serpent " built at Ledehammers near Nidaros in Norway, " a man called Thorberg Skavhogg was the shipwright, but there were many others on the work, some to fell trees, some to hew them and some to make nails and some to carry timber." [26]

Shipbuilding was facilitated by " a rich and comprehensive production of iron implements, of which the iron-axe was the most important." [27] Iron was extracted partly from ordinary ore, but mostly from the so-called bog-ores. The art of extracting iron, derived from the Romans, " attained

[24] *Ibid.*, p. 38.

[25] S. C. Gilfillan, *op. cit.*, p. 48.

[26] *Heimskringla, Saga of Olav Tryggvason*, 95. The *Gulathings Law* (306) distinguishes between stave-smiths (*stafnasmidir*) and board fitters (*filungar*). The former, who hewed the keel and the boards, were paid two oras per day, and the latter, who joined the boards, received one ora per day.

[27] A. W. Brøgger, *Ancient Emigrants* (Oxford, 1929), pp. 12-13.

its highest point of perfection in the seventh and eighth centuries and the viking age." The wealth of iron in the North in viking times is shown by a comparison of " the profuse collection of iron implements found in the grave of a well-to-do Northman of the eighth or ninth century— axes, knives, drills, bits and the like—with the poor equipment of iron implements on one of the farms of Charles the Great in the same period." [28]   Iron was so rare in the Carolingian Empire that " on one of Charlemagne's domains there were to be found only two axes, two spades, two gimlets, a hatchet and a plane.   A hundredweight of iron was then worth fifty times as much as it fetched at the end of the nineteenth century, and the smith was the most honoured of technicians.   A breast plate was worth six oxen . . . and a bit cost more than a horse." [29]

The outstanding characteristic of the viking ships was their greater effective radius of operation, made possible by a more extensive use of the sail and the wind for motive power.   This technological development was in turn closely tied up with institutional forces in the North, which were absent or not equally strong in other parts of Europe.   The Roman ships, for example, were almost entirely slave-propelled.   But slaves as a source of energy were bulky; besides officers and sailors, two watches of oarsmen had to be carried along, with provisions for all.   The result was that there were marked limits to the number of warriors and the size of the cargoes.[30]   The effective radius of action of the Roman ships was therefore decidedly circumscribed.

In the North, on the other hand, slave-power was less abundant and the institutions different.   The slaves tilled the

[28] *Ibid.*, p. 16.

[29] P. Boissonnade, *Life and Work in Medieval Europe* (London, 1927), p. 106.

[30] Sidney A. Reeve, " Ship Evolution and Social Evolution," *The Geographical Review*, vol. xxiii (1933), p. 64.

soil and performed the chores on the farms, while the sea was primarily looked upon as the free man's domain. Somehow, whether as a result of the institutional setting or by mere chance,[31] this technological change from slave-power to sail was hit upon, giving the Northmen a decided advantage on the sea. With the increased use of sails, skillful navigation and daring seamanship became more important than rowing-strength based upon the number of slaves available for the oar-posts. The Northmen became the foremost seafarers of the times, and far-away shores lay open to them.[32] This technological advantage was in a large measure responsible for the virtually sustained success that the vikings enjoyed. Without it, their speedy and unpredictable movements along the various shores of Western Europe would have been impossible. Conversely, the chief weakness of Charlemagne's empire was the lack of " half of

[31] There is an interesting saga account indicating how improvements in shipbuilding technique came about. One morning King Olav Tryggvason and Thorberg, his master-shipwright, walked down to the shore where the "Long Serpent" was being built. " The carpenters were there before them, but all were standing idle, with their arms crossed. The king asked ' what was the matter ', they said the ship was destroyed; for somebody had gone from stem to stem and cut one deep notch after the other down one side of the planking." The king became angry and swore that the man should die who had "thus destroyed the vessel out of envy," and promised a great reward for the one who found him out. "I can tell you, king," said Thorberg, "who did this piece of work. I did it myself." " Then Thorberg went and chipped the planks until the deep notches were all smoothed and made even with the rest; and the king and all present declared that the ship was much handsomer on the side of the hull which Thorberg had chipped, and bade him shape the other side in the same way, and gave him great thanks for the improvement " (*Heimskringla, Saga of Olav Tryggvason*, 95).

[32] Referring to the early trips to England, one of the commentators states that before they actually occurred " no one thought that such voyages would be possible " ("*nec ejus modi navigium fieri posse putabatur*"). *Mon. Alciniana*, ed. *Jaffe, No. 28*. Quoted from Steenstrup, *op. cit.*, vol. ii, p. 7.

all power, namely sea-power." [33]   Without a fleet with which
to protect his shores, Charlemagne's lookout towers and alert
guards were helpless.   The Carolingians had to flee to save
their lives while the Northmen, in their absence, " peace-
fully " looted the towns and sanctuaries.   Only when the
potential victims had ships of their own, as in the case of
the Moors and King Alfred, were they able to meet the
vikings on equal terms.

The superior ship constituted the chief advantage of the
Northmen.   In addition, in part as a result of the development of the ship, there had evolved certain forms of organization and modes of attack which likewise were of considerable importance.

The viking enterprises assumed different forms, in adap-
tation to the conditions of the various regions that were
being exploited.   The Northmen who engaged in piracy and
trade formed relatively small units or bands, employing
from one to a dozen ships.   There were also individual
vikings who specialized in marauding.   This is brought out
by the story about Sweyn Asleifsson of ·Orkney, who as late
as 1171, in the reign of Henry II, " fared a sea-roving."
" Sweyn had in the spring hard work, and made them
lay down very much seed, and looked much after it himself.
But when that toil was ended, he fared away every spring
on a viking voyage, and harried about among the southern
isles and Ireland, and came home after midsummer.   That
he called spring-viking.   Then he was at home until the
corn-fields were reaped down, and the grain seen to and
stored.   Then he fared away on a viking voyage, and then
he did not come home till the winter was one month off,
and that he called his autumn-viking." [34]   Numerous pass-

---

[33] L. von Ranke, *Französische Geschichte, vornehmlich in sechzehnten
und siebzehnten Jahrhundert* (Leipzig, 1868), vol. iv, pp. 520, 533.

[34] *Orkneyinga saga*, 105.

ages in the saga literature suggest that this account, which depicts viking activity in the Scandinavian colony of the Orkneys, may be looked upon as an illustration of the type of enterprise engaged in by the earlier vikings of Scandinavia proper. In many places, such as Man, Shetland and the Faroes, practices which characterized the very first phases of the viking activities remained in vogue long after the movement as a whole had gone through the various stages of warfare on land and conquests, and had ceased to be a phenomenon of real consequence in the more important regions of northern Europe.

There were vikings who boasted that they never slept under a sooty ceiling nor ate at a table, and that their only home was the sea. There were those who, for some reason or other, had been exiled from their home provinces. These Northmen who were engaged in the viking enterprises on a full-time basis were called sea-kings [35] or "ness-vikings," because they generally established their headquarters in a fortress on a "*nes*" or peninsula, on a cliff-island or at some other equally advantageous point.

Building the ships and equipping them for the expeditions overseas required capital in such amounts as could be raised only by the wealthy or those having wealthy connections.[36]

---

[35] J. A. A. Worsaae, *Den norske Erøbring af England og Normandiet* (Copenhagen, 1863), p. 26.

[36] There were also other types of equipment used. Foremost among these was the sword. Archaeological finds suggest that the single-edged, pointed sword was still in use among the Northmen during the viking age, but the two-edged heavy blade was more common. As a rule the swords were of the prevailing continental type made in Germany. Those produced in the North itself were inferior to those from the outside, as "French" and "Flemish" swords are highly praised in the saga literature. "Their swords are broad, with wavy lines, and of Frankish make," states Ibn Fadlan (*Ibn Fadlan's Account,...,* p. 56). See Jan Petersen, "*De norske vikingesverd*" in *Videnskabssellskabets Skrifter,*

The less wealthy had to attach themselves to these leaders on the best terms obtainable. The profession of both warrior and merchant viking was on the whole open only to free men. The contingent that followed a viking leader to the fields overseas consisted therefore chiefly of the free men of his own household and the immediate countryside. Each man provided his own food or contributed his share to the common board of the group. No fixed wages were paid or guaranteed. Each participant served at his own risk and was given a certain percentage of the returns, depending upon the size of his contribution or the value of his services. The contract, as in the case of agreements generally, was sealed by a handclasp; hence the persons who were to contribute only their services came to be called " hands." [37]

Not all viking ventures were privately launched. Many of the larger campaigns were undertaken by the *leding* or *ledung,* an organization sponsored and controlled by the kings.[38] The *leding* consisted of a large fleet, to which each *hundare, härad* or *skeppslag*—depending upon the region of the North—contributed a definite number of ships, and a definite number of warriors and oarsmen for each ship.[39]

Christiania, 1919; and G. Gjessing, *Norsk Hist. Tidsskrift, 2 R., 8 B.* The battle-axe, which had a singularly long handle, was also a common weapon of the times. The Greeks referred to the Northmen as the " axe-bearing barbarians from Thule," and the Varangians at Constantinople had an axe in their coat of arms. The vikings also possessed spears, bows and arrows, and shields, as well as other forms of protective armor.

[37] E. Hertzberg, *op. cit.,* p. 9.

[38] The origin of the *leding* is traced to Svealand, whose people had been marauders in the Baltic lands since before the days of Tacitus (H. Schück, *op. cit.,* vol. i, p. 309). When the *Svear* subdued the *Götar,* the *leding* was extended to Götaland; later this form of organization was also adopted in Denmark and Norway (H. Schück, *op. cit.,* vol. i, p. 310).

[39] The subdivisions of Svealand and Gotland were called *hundare,* earlier *hund.* These words mean "mass" or "groups of people" and included no doubt the territory of several clans or families. In Denmark, southern

The activities of the *leding* were generally seasonal; in Svealand, according to the provincial law code of Uppland, the *leding* was called out each year by the *thing* held at Candlemasstime.

As had been indicated in an earlier chapter, the leaders of the larger viking enterprises were generally members of the high-born class. This applies both to the private ventures and the *leding*. In certain cases the positions of leadership became hereditary, since the son or the sons of a deceased king or jarl often were called upon to guide the destinies of a certain group of vikings. But inheritance of positions of leadership was not very rigid. In 871 the Danish army in England was divided into two divisions, one led by King Bagsaec and King Halfdane, and the other by a number of jarls. In 875, three kings, Gudrun, Oscylet and Anwind, are mentioned as leaders of the viking forces. The treaty of 912 between the Varangian-Russian ruler Oleg and the Emperors Leo and Alexander of Constantinople, suggests that there existed a "comitatus" or a system of co-adjutors among the vikings in Russia.[40] Similar conditions prevailed in England, as shown by the agreement between King Aethelred and Olav, Jostein and Gudmund.[41]

Sweden and Götaland, the subdivisions were called *herred* or *härad,* meaning "host of people" (Sven Tunberg, *Skandinaviens äldsta politiska indelning,* pp. 203-207). Each *hundare* or *härad* was divided into *skeppslag,* i. e., a territory which must furnish and equip one ship. Gotland, a late accession to Svealand, was not thus divided, however, as "the whole land" was to contribute seven ships. On the other hand, although not divided into *hundare,* the new settlements in northern Sweden were divided directly into *skeppslag.* (H. Schück, *op. cit.,* vol. i, p. 310).

[40] The treaty of 912 reads as follows: "We of Russian birth, Karl, Ingjald, Farulf, etc. are being sent by Oleg, Grand Prince of Kiev, and by all his glorious bojars," etc. (*Russian Primary Chron.,* 912).

[41] After the battle of Maldon in 991, King Aethelred bought peace from the Northmen for 10,000 pounds of silver. The treaty reads as follows: "This is the peace which King Aethelred and his whole witan

Occasionally several viking leaders joined forces.[42]   No less than six different viking armies participated in the siege of Paris in 886, and several viking chieftains time and again ravaged or fought together both on English soil and elsewhere where the Northmen were active.   But there were also instances of very keen competition between different viking bands.   If a viking force tried to enter a region that formerly had been the prerogative of a certain viking leader or succession of leaders, such attempts were challenged; witness the battle between the Danes and the Norwegians at Collingford Loch in 851.   As a rule, however, such ruinous competition was avoided among the various viking units, and voluntary arrangements were often made for campaigns that were too difficult to be undertaken by one leader, single-handed.   Harald Ironhead is said to have suggested to Sigismund, his foe, that they become friends and discontinue fighting each other.   " The men of both sides thought well of this and persuaded them to make peace."   With combined efforts they " raided far and wide in the summers, and few could stand against them." [43]

The sagas describe a large viking combine which had its headquarters at Jomsborg, in the Baltic, reputedly a large stronghold capable of holding 300 ships at anchor within the confines of the harbor.[44]   Very strict rules governed

made with the army which Anlauf, Justian and Gudmund, Stegitan's son, led." It was this situation that prompted Henric of Huntingdon to remark that a state of confusion seemed to prevail among the Danes in Northumbria with regard to their form of leadership, as at one time they would have one king and at another time several kings. See Steenstrup, *op. cit.*, vol. i, p. 288.

[42] See *Heimskringla, Saga of Harald Fairhair*, 22.

[43] *Saga of the Faroe Islanders*, 20. This saga deals with the period during which Hakon Jarl ruled in Norway, or from 976 to 995.

[44] The story about the organization of the Jomsvikings is found in a number of sagas, but most elaborately described in the *Jomsvikingasaga*. See also Thorstein Veblen, "An Early Experiment in Trusts " (1904), republished in *The Place of Science in Modern Civilization* (New York, 1919), pp. 504-507.

the admission to and conduct in this organization. The viking must be at least eighteen years of age, but not more than fifty. He must have shown exceptional bravery in combat. Private retention of booty was prohibited. No one was allowed to remain away from the fortress more than three days in succession, without first having secured special permission. No women were permitted to enter the fortress. Unlike the location of most of the places of note mentioned in the saga literature, that of the site of Jomsborg has not yet been definitely established, and as a result, the historical existence of the combine has been questioned.[45] In view of the recent discovery near Grobin in Latvia, however, of the site of Seeburg, a town mentioned in Rimbert's *Life of Anskar* and a number of sagas, it seems possible that the site of Jomsborg may eventually also be found.[46]

In places the Northmen constructed stockades of timber and earthworks which were used as bases from which to plunder the adjacent territory.[47] But of much greater significance in their operations was the mobility of their forces. Like a whirlwind the viking ships would swoop down upon some coast, and having attained their objective, they would leave as suddenly as they had arrived. The same swiftness characterized their military activities on land. Even after a protracted period of siege and warfare, they would march

---

[45] See Sofus Larsen, *Aarbøger f. nord. Oldkyndighed og Historie,* III *Række,* 17 and 18 (1927 and 1928); *Sitzungsberichte der preussischen Akad. der Wissenschaften,* 1924, p. 176; T. D. Kendrick, *op. cit.,* p. 180; and Lauritz Weibull, *Kritiska undersökelser i Nordens historia omkring år 1000* (Lund, 1911), p. 176.

[46] See B. Nerman, *Nordisk Tidskrift, 1934;* Finnur Jonsson, *Dansk Hist. Tidsskrift, 8 R., 3 B.* (1912); and Sven Tunberg, *Svensk Hist. Tidskrift, 1911.*

[47] Many of these earthworks still exist along the coasts of Western Europe and are readily distinguished by the archaeologists from those of Roman or British origin.

straight across England, for example, with astonishing rapidity.

In 866, according to the Anglo-Saxon Chronicle, a viking army landed in East Anglia and at once set about to procure horses for the impending campaign further inland.[48] This even marked the inauguration of a new technique of warfare in England, which proved so effective that within two decades it was the generally accepted method everywhere.[49] It consisted in securing all the available horses in the district to which the invaders came; the larger the number of horses that were obtained, the greater was the speed of the army. The Northmen brought no horses from their homeland, but acquired them where and when they were needed. At times horses were greatly in demand; and when the Northmen found it inconvenient to take them by force, they would buy them.[50] Occasionally they would transport horses from one field of operation to another. The Anglo-Saxon Chronicle states that in the year 893 " the great army . . . came to Boulogne and was there shipped so that they in one voyage made the transit with horses and all."

The actual fighting, however, was done on foot; not even the leaders fought on horseback. We read that at Brunanburh King Aethelstan " left the battlefield while his men pursued the fugitives. He mounted his horse and rode back to the burh." A viking army was divided into " *fylkingar*," each of which comprised men who as a rule came from the same region in the North. A " *fylking* " was divided into " *hundrud*," (singular *hundrad*) of 120 men each. In combat the Northmen employed the traditional wedge formation;

[48] "A great heathen army came out of the land of the East Angles and there was the army ahorsed."

[49] Fletcher Pratt, " The Cavalry of the Vikings," *The Cavalry Journal*, vol. 42 (1933), p. 20.

[50] See Steenstrup, *op. cit.*, vol. i, p. 358.

i. e., two men in front, then four, then six, and so on. To one of the commentators their manner of warfare resembled more a slaughtering of animals than an attack upon humans.[51] They "raised foreign barbarous shouts, and blew warlike trumpets."[52] One of their war-cries was " *Tur aie!* " (Thor help us!).[53]

Emblems and banners played an important rôle in the viking armies.[54] The *Prose Edda* states that if, in the absence of the king or the jarls, the banner is carried in front of *hersar* or *lendirmenn,* this is a token that the latter are the leaders of the army. Both a large flag or banner and a figure attached to a staff were used. The victims considered the flags, which generally were blood-colored, ghastly to behold.[55]

The records suggest that the Northmen showed marked resourcefulness in combat. Dudo St. Quentin relates how Rollo and his men on one occasion were hard pressed by a pursuing troop on horseback. The terrain was level, offering no natural protection which would help them to check the pursuers. But the vikings cut down some of their stolen cattle, partly skinned the animals, and built a makeshift stockade, turning the bloody parts toward the approaching enemy. The horses of the latter balked when

---

[51] Pertz, *Scriptores*, vol. i, p. 592. An illustration showing the artistic bent of the Northmen in devising types of cruelty is found in the practice of "cutting the blood eagle" (Old Norse *blodörn*), a form of sacrifice to Odin, God of Warfare. It consisted of the severing of the ribs from the backbone, spreading them out to resemble the wings of an eagle, and the pulling out of the lungs from the opening while the victim was still alive. See *Blodörn* in Cleasby and Vigfusson, *An Icelandic-English Dictionary.*

[52] *Three Fragments* (O'Donovan's ed.), p. 165.

[53] *Roman de Rou*, vol. ii, p. 32. Quoted from Steenstrup, *op. cit.*, vol. i, p. 363.

[54] See *Flateyabók*, ii, 72-73.

[55] Pertz, *op. cit.*, vol. i, p. 498.

they came to this barrier. Aided by the delay, the vikings were able to get to their ships.

" The vikings . . . possessed the best military brains of their age," writes a student of military science. They " did about as they pleased," because "they held all the trumps. They were well-armored professional soldiers, of high mobility, with good scouting services, against hastily raised levies." [56] Their movements were rapid and unpredictable, and tactically they were in a position to deliver a considerable blow against an enemy formation and to follow it up instantly with a close-range infantry attack.

The Northmen often found it difficult to secure supplies and sustenance for their expeditionary forces. Ibn-al-Coutia states that the vikings who in 844 plundered Seville refused any other form of tribute than clothing and food stuffs.[57] Under the year of 894, the Anglo-Saxon Chronicle, referring to a contingent of vikings in England, says that " they were distressed for want of food, and had eaten a great part of their horses and the other [horses] had died of hunger." Throughout the autumn the vikings were engaged in storing up provisions for the ensuing winter, and they were generally on hand to relieve the farmers of the trouble of gathering the harvest. In 896, according to the Anglo-Saxon Chronicle, Alfred the Great took his army to the vicinity of the viking headquarters in order to prevent the Danes from confiscating the yield of the fields. Secondary units, or " quartermaster corps," followed the main armies both on land and on the sea.[58]

Outposts were established in the various regions to which the Northmen came. Foremost of these were Kiev and

---

[56] Fletcher Pratt, *op. cit.*, p. 20.

[57] Steenstrup, *op. cit.*, vol. i, p. 372.

[58] *Ser. Rer. Dan.*, ii, 55; *Guill. Apul., Maratori*, v, p. 276. From Steenstrup, *op. cit.*, vol. i, p. 372.

Novgorod, which in the course of time developed into regular viking domains and provinces. Even during the early part of the period of viking aggression, the Northmen maintained establishments at both these points for the building and repairing of ships.[59]   Similarly, Man, the Hebrides, the Orkneys and other islands in Northwestern Europe became viking strongholds in the West. Walcheren served as the headquarters for the operation in the region around the Maas, the Scheldt and the Rhine. Oscellus became the center for the region of the Seine and its tributaries, and Noirmoutiers for the territory of Nantes, Tours and Orleans.[60]   In the Black Sea, the islands of St. Gregorius and St. Aetherius were made to serve as depots from which expeditions went out to Greece and the Near East. The Greeks were fully aware of the dangers to them of the proximity of such viking centers, and in their treaty with Igor in 947 they stipulated that the Northmen henceforth were not to spend the winter at the estuary of the Dnieper, but were to return home to Russia each fall.[61]

[59] Constantine Porphyrogenetus, *op. cit.*, ch. 9.

[60] Steenstrup, *op. cit.*, vol. ii, p. 249.

[61] *The Russian Primary Chron.*; Steenstrup, *op. cit.*, vol. i, p. 355; and T. J. Arne, *Det stora Svitjod* (Stockholm, 1914), p. 40.

CHAPTER VI

OPERATIONS IN RUSSIA AND CONSTANTINOPLE

THE Northmen themselves, when referring to their various regions of operation, spoke of "*Austrveg*" (to the East) and "*Vestrveg*" (to the West). The "eastern way" led to the East Baltic region, to Russia, Constantinople and the Near East. The "western way" led to the British Isles, the Carolingian Empire and Southwestern Europe. This chapter will deal with the operations in the East, while the following two will be devoted to the expeditions to the West.

Archaeological finds have shown that Swedes dwelt on the eastern shores of the Baltic early in the Christian era.[1] Trips eastward, made by Swedes and other Northmen, are described in such widely independent sources as Rimbert's *Life of Anskar* and Snorre's *Heimskringla*.[2] According to the *Ynglinga Saga*, there was a Swedish "*sysla*" or taxpaying district in Courland or in Estonia in the early part of the viking period.[3] As late as the thirteenth century, there were provisions in the law code of Västergötland concerning the rights of inheritance which differentiated between "Greecefarers" and "Swedes at home," suggesting that expeditions to the East were rather common even among the people of Western Sweden.[4] At the beginning of the viking

---

[1] Montelius, *Finsk Tidskrift*, vol. 44 (1898), p. 95.

[2] B. Nerman, *Die Verbindungen Zwischen Skandinavien und dem Ostbaltikum in der jüngeren Eisenzeit* (Stockholm, 1929), p. 51.

[3] H. Schück, *Studier i Ynglingatal* (Upsala, 1910), p. 165.

[4] A. Munthe, *Sjömaktens inflytande på Sveriges historia, Marinlitteraturföreningens arbeten, no. 24* (Stockholm, 1922), p. 22.

period, the town of Ladoga, then called Aldeigjaborg, was the center for the activities of the fur-trading Swedes in this region. From Aldeigjaborg the Swedes had already by this time made trading journeys as well as marauding expeditions through the interior of Russia to the Caspian Sea, Constantinople and the Balkan region, where they obtained precious metals and many of their luxuries, such as wine, spices, fancy cloth and ornaments.

The following citation from the *Heimskringla* gives a vivid picture of a viking leader at work in the Baltic. " Eric [the Jarl] took counsel to get himself ships and to go raiding to win goods for himself and his men. He sailed first to Gotland and lay off there for a long time in the summer and waylaid either merchant ships which were sailing to the land, or viking ships; sometimes he went up on land and harried far about the coast. . . . After that Eric the Jarl sailed south to Vendland, and outside Stauren [5] he met several viking ships and fell to battle with them. Eric had the victory and slew the vikings. . . . In the autumn Eric the Jarl sailed back to Sweden and was there another winter. But in the spring he made his ships ready and sailed then to the eastern countries. And when he came to King Valdemar's kingdom he began to harry and slay folk and to burn everything wherever he went, and he laid waste the land. He came to Aldeigjaborg and beset the town until he won it, slew many folk and broke down and burned the whole town; he then went far and wide in Gardarik [6] with the shield of war. . . . Eric the Jarl was altogether five summers on this expedition; and when he came to Gardarik, he

---

[5] Stauren is supposed to be the southernmost point of the island of Femern, now Staver, south of Staberdorp. See *Heimskringla*, E. Monsen's ed. (Cambridge, 1932), p. 183, note 3.

[6] Gardarik was the viking term for the present day Russia. The Old Norse " *Gardariki* " means " the land of farms."

went with the shield of war all over Adalsysla [7] and Eysysla and there he took four viking ships from the Danes and slew all the men. Eric the Jarl went to Denmark, when he had been one winter in Sweden [and married the daughter of the Danish King]. In the winters Eric was in Denmark and sometimes in Sweden, but in the summers he was harrying." [8]

The much-discussed question of the origin of the alleged founders of the Russian state we propose to pass over with a mere mention.[9] With a few dissenting voices, it is now held by the scholars that the Rhos or Russ were Northmen, more particularly Swedes.[10] In 859, according to the Russian Primary Chronicle,[11] more commonly known as the Nestor Chronicle, " the Varangians from beyond the sea imposed tribute upon the Chuds, the Slavs," and other tribes in Russia, collecting a squirrel-skin from each hearth. The chronicle states that this was the first appearance of Northmen in Russia, but other records indicate that the Swedes had had contacts with Constantinople long before this time.[12]

[7] Adalsysla was the Old Norse name for the mainland opposite the island of Osel, the latter being called Eysysla. By " *sysla* " was meant a district, primarily a fiscal division. See Schück, *op. cit.*, pp. 151-153.

[8] *Saga of Olav Tryggvason*, 89-91.

[9] Thus there have arisen two groups, the pro-Scandinavian and the anti-Scandinavian. The attempts of the latter to disprove that Russia was founded by Rurik have yielded but meager results. B. Nerman, of the former group, tersely states: " *Rurik grundede den russischen Staat*," *op. cit.*, p. 49. See also T. J. Arne, *op. cit.*, p. 63.

[10] See V. O. Kluychevsky, *A History of Russia* (London, 1911), vol. i, pp. 58-59.

[11] *The Russian Primary Chronicle*, generally attributed to Nestor, is a compilation of several different manuscripts. See Kluychevsky, *op. cit.*, vol. i, pp. 18-27. For an English version see S. H. Cross' translation, published in *Harvard Studies and Notes in Philology and Literature*, vol. xii (1928), pp. 75-320.

[12] Thus, already in 839, Swedish ambassadors came to the court of the Greek Emperor. Upon leaving for home, these Rhos received a letter of recommendation to Emperor Louis the Pious. When the latter learned

In the year 862 the payment of tribute was discontinued, and the Varangians were driven across the sea. The inhabitants found, however, that they were unable to govern themselves successfully. " There was no law among them, but tribe rose against tribe and began to make war one against another." Envoys were sent " across the sea to the Varangians, or the Rus, for so were the Varangians called," with the following message: " Our whole land is great and rich, but there is no order in it. Come to rule and reign over us! " In response to this request, three brothers, Rurik, Sineus and Truvor, " went across the sea with all their kinsfolk." Upon the death of his brothers, Rurik, who had settled in Novgorod, assumed the government of their district also. The chronicle further states that " the Russian land, Novgorod, was called after these Varangians; they are the Novgorodians of Varangian descent; previously the Novgorodians were Slavs." [13]

that they were Swedes, he became suspicious and threw them into prison until he had satisfied himself that they were not spies who were reconnoitering for some nefarious purpose. See Vilhelm Thomsen, *The Relation between Ancient Russia and Scandinavia and the Origin of the Russian State* (Oxford, 1877), p. 40.

[13] The Greeks referred to the district of Kiev as the "territory of the Rus," and the "men of Rus" were also called " Scandinavians " (Liudprand, *Antapodosis*, v. 15). With the lapse of time, the term came to denote members of the upper classes in Russian cities, regardless of Slavic or Nordic origin. The word " Rus," as a term denoting the inhabitants of Russia, is apparently derived from " *Ruotsi*," the Finnish appellation of raiders and colonists from eastern Sweden (S. H. Cross, Introduction, *op. cit.*, p. 133). The Estonian term is " *Rots.*" " *Ruotsi*" and " *Rots* " are derived from " *rodsmen*," meaning " rowers " or " seafarers " who came from Roslagen, a district along the coast just north of Stockholm. In Roslagen as well as elsewhere along the western coast of the Baltic, the shore-line was divided into rowing-units, the duty of which it was to provide a certain number of ships fully equipped and manned for the expeditions undertaken by the king at Upsala. By Roslagen was thus meant the district in which the rowing-law was in effect. See R. Ekblom, *Arch. d'Etudes Orientales*, vol. xi, p. 6. *Cf.*. also

The implication, however, that an unanimous invitation was extended to the Northmen is highly improbable. It is more likely that only one tribe, which was getting the worst of it in the inter-tribal strife, asked the Varangians to come in to check the invasions of neighboring peoples. The Northmen remained, and in the North, Russia became known as *Svithiod hin Mikla* (Great Sweden) while Sweden proper was called Svithiod Minor.[14] In the beginning, the Northmen lived as a ruling class of foreigners, but it was not long before the process of assimilation was at work. This process, however, was not a rapid one. Arne, the archaeologist, concludes that the Swedish language was spoken or was understood in many parts of Russia throughout the viking period.[15]

On the basis of archaeological studies, Raudonikas divides the viking activities in Russia into two periods.[16] The earlier period, which came to a close in the middle of the ninth century, was characterized by Swedish expeditions. The invaders plundered and exacted tributes as they went along on their trips down the Dnieper and the Volga, and brought captive Slavs to Constantinople and other Near East

H. Schück, *Svenska folkets historia*, vol. i, p. 203. In opposition to these views, it has been adduced that the term "Rus" was used by the people of Russia even before the arrival of the Varangians to denote the inhabitants of a district in the Caucasian region. (E. Konig, *Zeitschrift d. deut. morgenl. Gesellschaft*, vol. 70, p. 22). However, the Scandinavian origin of "Rus" is now well established.

[14] *Heimskringla, Ynglinga Saga*, I.

[15] T. J. Arne, "*Östeuropas och Nordbalkans förhistoria*," in *De fornhistoriske Tider i Europa*, ed. by Knud Friis Johansen (Copenhagen, 1927), p. 451.

[16] W. J. Raudonikas, *Die Normannen der Wikingerzeit und das Ladogagebiet* (Stockholm, 1930), pp. 138 *et seq*. Arne adds a third period by subdividing Raudonikas' last period into two, the first of which (comprising the closing decades of the ninth and the first half of the tenth century) he calls the period of colonization. (*Det stora Svitjod* and other contributions).

markets. In the later period, from the middle of the ninth to the beginning of the eleventh century, the Slavs offered increasingly effective opposition to the exploiters, occasionally by hiring other Varangians or Scandinavians to fight the invaders. This opposition made plunder difficult and served to further organized trade. The vikings established permanent posts along the river high-ways of Russia and gained a dominant position among the Slavs. At these posts or centers, of which Kiev (Old Norse *Kœnogardr*) was the foremost, they pursued a considerable barter trade, in which furs constituted the most important commodity.[17] During the later period the Varangians and the natives gradually merged, and the Russian principalities became increasingly Slavonian in character. But the vikings plundered and exacted tribute also in the last period; and for several centuries, many Varangians continued to go to Russia to seek their fortune.[18]

By the beginning of the ninth century, the Swedes had established a politico-military stronghold in Säborg, or Seeburg, in present-day Latvia.[19] Novgorod (Old Norse *Holmgardr*), called by Nestor a " Varangian City," was an important trading mart which long retained the characteristics that the Northmen had given to it. In the tenth century, avowedly under viking dominance, Novgorod was one of the centers of Russian commerce. Merchants from the North, notably Gotlanders and Swedes, came here in large numbers, and even Norwegians and Icelanders are mentioned as slave-traders in Novgorod and Constantinople.[20] The

---

[17] Raudonikas, *op. cit.*, pp. 136-141.

[18] *Ibid.*; Arne, *Östeuropas och Nordbalkans förhistoria*, pp. 450 *et seq.*; *cf.* H. Schück, *Svenska folkets historia*, vol. i, p. 208.

[19] *Life of Anskar*, ch. 27. The location of Seeburg has been established at Grobin, near Libau. See B. Nerman, *Nordisk Tidskrift*, 1934.

[20] *Cf. Hrafnkels Saga*, ch. 5.

chief commodities dealt in were furs and wax, and silk and fancy cloth from the Orient. About the year 1015, the Northmen merchants had their own gild house (Old Norse *farmannagardr*) in the city, and later there was a gild house exclusively for Gotlanders.

The route that the Northmen took to Novgorod led over the Gulf of Finland, up the river Neva into Lake Ladoga, and then partly up the river Volkhov to Novgorod. From Novgorod there were two highways through the interior of Russia, one leading to the Black Sea and Constantinople, and the other to the Caspian Sea. On their way to Constantinople (Old Norse *Mikligardr,* i. e., the great city) the Northmen would go from Novgorod up the Lovat almost to its source, carry their boats to the S. Dvina, and then, after a short trip up that river, again carry them to the Dnieper. Going down the Dnieper, they reached Kiev, the largest trading mart of Russia. From Kiev they would continue further down the river, bringing their boats overland past the seven falls of the Dnieper.[21] From the mouth of the Dnieper they sailed to the Greek colonies and to Constantinople, where this main route of trade generally terminated. The eastern-most route in Russia went from Novgrorod by the way of the Eyas and the Mologa to the Volga and thence to the Caspian Sea and the Saracen East. The chief trading centers on this route were Bulgar, in the interior, and Itil, on the Volga delta, approximately where the present-day Astrakhan is situated. The Northmen brought furs, slaves and amber and received in return " white, round Dirhims ", i. e., silver coins. The Volga route was closed in the eleventh century, but the route to Constantinople maintained its importance throughout that century and even later. In addition to the two main routes, there were also other ap-

[21] Constantine Porphyrogenitus, *op. cit.,* 9; T. J. Arne, *Det stora Svitjod,* pp. 138-140; Kendrick, *op. cit.,* pp. 151-152.

proaches to the interior of Russia, the chief one being by the way of the river S. Dvina. This latter route appears to have been used almost exclusively by Gotlanders.

In the East, as elsewhere, the desire for plunder was present in strong relief. " Boldly they sought gold in far-off lands and in the East fed the eagle " [22] testifies a Swedish rune-stone. The East-viking was less of a " sea brigand " than his brother the West-viking; the proximity of the sea and the fact that it afforded the only means by which he could reach England and the shores of Northwestern Europe made the West-viking take to the sea.[23] That large hordes seldom went to and fro in Russia, plundering towns and monasteries, as was the custom in the West, may be ascribed to the fact that there were few places of concentrated wealth in Russia. In Persia, along the Caspian Sea, and in the Near East generally, where such centers did exist, the traditional harrying flourished.

Commerce occupied a preponderant position in the viking activities in the east, but the records also tell of formidable attacks and large-scale plunder. Thus in 860, as a result of a quarrel between Greek merchants and Northmen traders, Askiold and Dir, the Varangian rulers of Kiev, went down the Dnieper with a fleet of 200 ships to the Black Sea and began ravaging its shores.[24] They sailed through the Bosphorus and cast anchor before the city of Constantinople. The suddenness with which they appeared brought

[22] The term "gold" was used in a broad sense to include wealth in general, and "to feed the eagle" meant to leave corpses on the battle field for the birds of prey.

[23] *Cf.* Klyuchevsky, *op. cit.*, p. 59.

[24] Kendrick, *op. cit.*, pp. 149-152. For a modification of this story, which is taken from Nestor or *The Russian Primary Chronicle*, see A. A. Vasiliev, *History of the Byzantine Empire*, vol. i, in *University of Wisconsin Studies in Social Science and History, no. 13* (Madison, 1928), p. 337.

general consternation among the people who, under the leadership of the Patriarch Photius, turned to religious ceremonies and implored the Holy Virgin to protect them. The Byzantine Chronicle states that, in answer to their prayers, a storm arose which destroyed the ships of the " barbarian Rhos."

Shortly after this attack, the Patriarch Photius wrote an encyclical to the oriental bishop, in which he mentioned the Rhos as " a people which surpasses all others in ferocity and blood-thirstiness. After having subdued the nations surrounding them, these Rhos have now carried their overweening pride so far as to raise their hands even against the Roman Emperor." [25] He also added that although they had abandoned their heathen and ungodly religion and been converted to Christianity, there was every reason to believe that this conversion had been only slight in extent and durability.[26]

About the year 880, Oleg (Helgi), Rurik's successor in Novgorod, captured Kiev, the key-city to the route to the Black Sea. Kiev became the capital of the Russian state and Oleg " the sovereign of a mighty political confederacy of town-provinces." All the eastern Slavonic tribes looked to him as their protector.[27]

In 907 Oleg made a great expedition against Constantinople, but the Greeks barricaded the Bosphorus.[28] The invaders thereupon went overland toward the city. Emperor Leo VI came to terms with the marauders, and a treaty was drawn up. Generous presents were bestowed upon Oleg and

---

[25] *Photii Epistolae* (*ed. Rich. Montacutius*, p. 58). Quoted from V. Thomsen, *Relation between Ancient Russia and Scandinavia*, ..., p. 24.

[26] *Cf.* Thomsen, *op. cit.*, p. 24.

[27] Kendrick, *op. cit.*, p. 151.

[28] " Oleg sallied forth by horse and by ship, and the number of his vessels was 2,000 " (*Russian Primary Chron.*).

his chieftains and gifts distributed among the members of the crews. The Emperor guaranteed these Russian vikings the right to enter their wares free of duty and to have their headquarters in Saint Mamas, a suburb of Constantinople, during their annual visits; in addition they were to have free maintenance during their stay.[29] The treaty further stipulated that the vikings must enter the city through one specified gate, and only in detachments of not more than fifty men.[30] Returning home from this expedition, " Oleg came to Kiev," the chronicle states, " bearing palls, gold, fruit and wine, along with every sort of adornment." [31]

[29] Oleg's warriors were not all Scandinavians, but included admixtures from various tribes under viking domination in Russia.
" The Russes proposed the following terms: ' The Russes who come hither shall receive as much grain as they require. Whosoever come as merchants shall receive supplies for six months, including bread, wine, meat, fish and fruit. Baths shall be prepared for them in any volume they require. When the Russes return homeward, they shall receive from your Emperor food, anchors, cordage, and sails, and whatever else is needful for the journey.' The Greeks accepted these stipulations, and the Emperors and all the courtiers declared: ' If Russes come hither without merchandise, they shall receive no provisions. Your Prince shall personally lay injunction upon such Russes as journey hither that they shall do no violence in the towns and throughout our territory. Such Russes as arrive here shall dwell in the Saint Mamas quarter. Our government will send officers to record their names, and they shall then receive their monthly allowance, first the natives of Kiev, then those from Chernigov, Pereyslavl, and the other cities. They shall not enter the city save through one gate, unarmed and fifty at a time, escorted by soldiers of the Emperor. They may purchase wares according to their requirements and tax-free " (*Russian Primary Chron.*, 907).

[30] *Cf.* S. Runciman, *The Emperor Romanus Lecapenus and his Reign* (Cambridge, 1929), p. 113.

[31] *The Russian Primary Chronicle* also states that " Oleg demanded that they should give to the troops on the two thousand ships twelve *grivni* per bench, and pay in addition the sums required for the various Russian cities; first Kiev, then Chernigov, Persyaslavi, Polotzk, Rostov, Lyubech, and the other towns. In these cities lived princes subject to Oleg." But nothing is said as to whether or not this demand was fulfilled.

Igor (Ingvarr), the son of Rurik and the successor of Oleg, also turned to marauding, although not on the extensive scale that characterized the viking operations in the West. In 941 he swept across the Black Sea with a large fleet to raid the city of Constantinople.[32]   But this attack was repelled chiefly because of the effective " Greek fire." [33]   Later he began to pillage in the provinces of Paphlagonia and Bithynia, where " they took no little booty on both sides of the sea." [34]   In the meantime the Greeks collected a large army with which they cut off the return of the viking expedition.   A fleet had also been gathered which, as in the earlier encounter, was under the command of Theophanes.   The ships of this fleet discharged " Greek fire," which caused such a panic among the men that large numbers of them were drowned and some even burned to death.   Only a few, among them Igor, escaped; those taken prisoners were later executed in the presence of the foreign ambassadors.[35]

Returning to Kiev, Igor sent to Sweden for fresh troops and in addition enlisted fighters from among several Slavic tribes and from the Pechenegs.   In 944 he set out for Constantinople " by ship and by horse."   Upon reaching the Danube, he was met by ambassadors of Emperor Romanus, who brought costly presents and induced Igor to accept a truce.   The latter, according to the chronicle, had a consultation with his chieftains, that " if the Emperor speaks

[32] Liudprand, *Antapodosis* (*Opus*, ed. Pertz, p. 139).   There are accounts to the effect that the fleet numbered 10,000 and even 15,000 ships, but this does not seem plausible.   *Cf.* Runciman, *op. cit.*, p. 111.

[33] The Emperor Romanus Lecapenus had fitted out fifteen old barques with apparatus for discharging a burning liquid, the exact nature of which is not known.   Presumably it was a composition of pitch, sulphur, naphtha and some other ingredients.   Through siphons the liquid was poured down upon the enemy.   See Arthur Marshall, *Explosives* (Philadelphia, 1917), vol. i, pp. 12-13.

[34] *The Russian Primary Chron.*

[35] Runciman, *op. cit.*, p. 112.

thus, what more do we desire beyond receiving gold, silver and palls without having to pay for them? Who knows who will be victorious, we or he? Who has the sea for his ally? For we are not marching by land, but through the depths of sea. Death lies in wait for us all." Igor heeded the chieftains and "bade the Pechenegs ravage Bulgaria. He, himself, after receiving from the Greeks gold and palls sufficient for his whole army, returned again and came to Kiev in his native land." [36] In 945 Greek ambassadors went to Kiev, and a treaty was made which "shows Russia as a well-organized state with large commercial interests, divided feudally between a number of cities under princes and princesses of the ruling and nobles houses, all under the Grand Prince of Kiev." [37] The treaty regulated prices and fines and also stipulated rules of conduct for the Russians while in Constantinople, as well as for the Greeks while in Russia.[38]

Igor fell in battle some years later and was succeeded by his son Svyatoslav, who was "the first prince to bear a genuinely Slavonian name." Since Svyatoslav was a minor, the realm was governed by Igor's widow Olga (Helga), who was "one of the wisest and most energetic of Russian rulers. She regulated the tribute and traveled round the country establishing depots for its collection." [39] Later, as Grand Prince, Svyatoslav made several expeditions to Bulgaria and Greece. After Svyatoslav's violent death in 972, his three sons fought over the succession. In the struggle Yaropolk was victorious, after Oleg had drowned and Vladimir had fled to "the land of the Varangians." Returning with an army, Vladimir overthrew his brother Yaropolk and

[36] *The Russian Primary Chron.*

[37] Runciman, *op. cit.*, p. 110.

[38] *The Russian Primary Chron.* (Cross' transl., pp. 160-162.) The rules agreed upon were very similar to those contained in the treaty of 907.

[39] Bernard Pares, *A History of Russia* (New York, 1928), p. 26.

thus became the ruler of the whole principality of Kiev. Vladimir became known not only as the great and insatiable fornicator, but also as the man who introduced Christianity into Russia.[40]

The Kiev settlement owed its beginning and importance to the trade route to the East that the Dnieper afforded. Of similar significance was the Volga route, over which the vikings went to the Caspian Sea and its surrounding territory. Throughout the ninth and tenth centuries, the Volga route was preferred to the Dnieper route by the traders from Gotland and the Swedish mainland, chiefly because of the fact that the Kiev vikings only reluctantly, and not without opposition, shared the use of their gateway to the commercial marts of the east.[41] But this route was also used for expeditions of plunder. Thus, in 914, or thereabouts, vikings are said to have sailed through the Sea of Azov into the Don. The vikings dragged their ships overland until they reached the Volga, whereupon they sailed downstream into the Caspian Sea. Here they harried, first on the coast of Persia and later in the region around Baku, " burning, plundering, and stealing children for the slave trade." Finally, however, the Moslems rose and, in a great battle near the mouth of the Volga, decisively defeated the Russians. Those who managed to escape perished on their homeward journey.

---

[40] " *fornicator immensus et crudelis* " (*M. G. H.*, Pertz, *Scriptores*, vol. iii, p. 859). Vladimir is said to have attacked the problem of Christianization in a very rational manner. Before making his choice, he requested representatives of various organized religions to appear before him and present the merits of their respective creeds. He rejected the Mohammedan faith on the ground that it demanded circumcision and abstinence from pork and wine. " Drinking," said he, " is the joy of the Russes. We cannot exist without that pleasure" (*Russian Primary Chron.*, Cross' transl., p. 184).

[41] See *Ibn Fadlan's Account.*

Dorn has given a thorough account of the viking expeditions to the Caspian Sea.[42] Raids were made in 880 and 910. In the course of the attack of 910, which took place along the Persian coast, the crews of sixteen Russian ships were annihilated. In 944 or 943, the raiders from the North sailed 200 miles up the River Kura to Berdaa and defeated a Mohammedan army. When a larger Moslem force was sent against them, they turned homeward. Although the vikings had lost many men, not only from fighting but also from an epidemic of dysentery, the material returns from this expedition were very great.[43]

There were also other raids to the Caspian Sea later on. There is the tradition about Ingvar Vittfarne who, after having gone to Semgallia in thirty ships, subduing the people and exacting a tribute from them, went to Russia in search of the source of that country's great rivers.[44] More than twenty rune-stones from various parts of Sweden bear inscriptions which refer to the activities of Ingvar and his men. One of these from the vicinity of the Gripsholm Castle, reads as follows: " Tola had this stone raised in memory of his son Harald, Ingvar's brother. Boldly they sought gold in far-off lands and in the East fed the eagle; died in South in Sarkland." [45]

The foremost Scandinavian stronghold on the Dnieper route was Kiev. In Novgorod, the other viking center in

[42] B. Dorn, *Caspia: Ueber die Einfälle der alten Russen in Tarbaristan, Mem. Acad. Imp. des Sciences*, St. Petersburg, *8 S.*, xxiii (1877), *1*.

[43] T. J. Arne, *Fornvännen, 1932*, p. 216.

[44] The name "vittfarne" means "widely traveled" and was used to denote a person who had traveled extensively.

[45] " Sarkland " was the name applied by the Northmen to the land of the Saracens, and the term was frequently used to denote any region inhabited by Mohammedans. This generally accepted explanation is not subscribed to by Arne, however, who believes that Sarkland stands for Sarkelland, the district that was protected by the fort or town of Sarkel in the land of the Khazars (*Fornvännen*, 1911, p. 23).

Russia, the Scandinavian characteristics were noticeable for centuries, in fact much longer than in Kiev. The fact that Nordic traditions and culture were retained in Novgorod for a long time may be ascribed to the relatively close proximity of the city to Scandinavia and the extensive commercial intercourse that was maintained up to the rise of the Hanseatic League.

It cannot be definitely ascertained when the Varangians first came to Constantinople to become members of the Emperor's Guard. Men from Thule were among the Federati already in the sixth century. The Greek historians allude to them and in cases even mention what the Northmen had told them about their country. In 911 there were Russians, clearly Northmen, taking part in a Greek expedition against Crete. Twenty years later more than 400 Russians (Northmen), in seven ships, were again enlisted by the Greeks for their expedition to southern Italy. In 949 about 600 of them in nine ships were a part of another Greek expedition to Crete. A goodly number were also found in the Byzantine army during the Mesopotamian wars about the middle of the tenth century.[46] The Icelandic sagas contain several passages about Icelanders being enlisted in the imperial guard at Constantinople.[47] The foremost of the Varangians was Harald Hardradi, whose deeds and merits popular tradition of the North built up to truly fantastic proportions.[48] Only twenty years old, Harald Hardradi embarked upon an expedition to Constantinople. He arrived at that city in 1034, was welcomed as the "King of Varangia", and was almost immediately invited to participate in a campaign against the Arabs in Asia Minor.[49] In war he displayed marked mili-

[46] Runciman, *op. cit.*, p. 144.

[47] *Laxdaela Saga, Saga of Burnt Nial* and the *Hrafnel Saga*.

[48] G. Storm, *Norsk Hist. Tidskrift*, 1 *Række, 4 Bind*, p. 386 and pp. 371-372.

[49] By Varangia was meant Scandinavia. See Storm, *op. cit.*, pp. 363-364.

tary ability. He was already on his way down the Jordan, harrying on both sides of the river as he went along, and in a position seriously to threaten Jerusalem itself, when peace was concluded. After a few years of service at the court, he and his men were sent on expeditions to Sicily and Bulgaria in 1038. His achievements in these campaigns gave him much prestige, and he was promoted to the third ranking position in the corps of attendants to the Emperor. After the revolution of 1042, he returned to the North and became king of Norway. For a long time other Northmen continued to enlist in the Varangian Guard, which, in spite of its relatively small size, exerted an extraordinary influence in the affairs of the State. The Greek writers commented on their foolhardy gallantries. Despite the many laudatory passages about their loyalty to the Emperor, their fidelity was not at all times unquestioned. There was a mutiny during the reign of Nicephorus III (1078-1081),[50] and Emperor Alexis in 1103 feared that they might shift their allegiance to Eric I of Denmark, who was paying the Emperor a visit in that year and who could speak their tongue.[51]

During the earlier period of the existence of the Varangian Guard, the Northmen, in addition to food and shelter, received from ten to fifteen gold solidi per month of service. There were also special prizes and grants available. As time went on, partly because of the honor that gradually became attached to it and partly because of the chances for lucrative rewards that it afforded, a commission in the guard came to command a price.

Sporadic raids had been made at various times upon the shores of the East Baltic, and there were periods during which these regions were completely under the domination

---

[50] Kendrick, *op. cit.*, p. 174.

[51] *Saxo Grammaticus* (J. Olrik's transl., iii-iv, p. 41).

of the Swedes. Raids were made both by Danes and Swedes in Courland about 854.[52] The Danes were unsuccessful, but the Swedes obtained " much gold, silver and arms," and in addition compelled the people to pay an annual tax for many years afterwards.

Numerous references in the sagas point to other instances of viking aggression in the East Baltic. Archaeological discoveries at the mouth of the Vistula indicate that the vikings were active also on the southern shores of the Baltic, presumably as participants in the once famous amber trade that went over this route.

The Northmen also found their way to the White Sea and to the coast of northern Russia. The trips to Bjarmaland, as this region was called, were primarily trading or exploitation voyages under the guise of the " shield of peace," although other motives have been given. Thus, Othere, the first of the Northmen to visit Bjarmaland, is said to have sailed northeast along the coast " in order to find out how far the land lay right north." [53] While an explorer's curiosity may have induced Othere to venture a trip to this unknown region, it appears that subsequent voyages were prompted by a desire for the valuable furs that the Bjarmians had to sell or give away.[54]

Geographically, the trips to Bjarmaland do not belong with the voyages over the " eastern way." The latter stood for expeditions eastward across the Baltic Sea, while Bjarmaland was reached by holding a northward or northeastward course. On the other hand, the character of the Bjarmaland voyages does not warrant their inclusion with the large scale marauding ventures directed against Western Europe. These voyages, specifically those dealing with England and Ireland, are to be considered in our next chapter.

[52] Rimbert, *Life of Anskar*, ch. 30; *Cf.* B. Nerman, *op. cit.*, p. 7.
[53] Alfred the Great, *op. cit.*, p. 8.
[54] See *supra*, p. 32.

CHAPTER VII

Operations in the Insular Regions of Northwestern Europe

On their way to the fields of operation in the insular regions of Northwestern Europe, the Northmen followed two main routes. One led from Norway and Iceland down along the west coast of Scotland through the Irish Sea to Dublin and Bristol. Referring to its trade relations, William of Malmesbury, one of the annalists, says about Bristol that the city was " a harbor for ships which came from Iceland, Norway and other overseas lands." [1] The other route went along the coast of the Continent down to the Strait of Dover and thence to London and York.

In viking times England's trade with other countries was carried on chiefly by foreigners. Merchants from the Low Countries, France and the German cities came to England in large numbers, bringing cloth, metal goods, wine and luxuries. Their return cargoes consisted mostly of wool, for which there was a great demand among the spinners and weavers in Flanders. Primarily because of the activities of these non-English traders, the Northmen were able to obtain in England such commodities as they coveted, notably wheat, honey and wine.[2] To England they brought furs, dried fish and other products of the North, and occasionally also some of the commodities that they had obtained in the

[1] The scope and character of the activities of the Northmen in Western Europe are revealed by the annals and chronicles of the exploited areas. Editions and translations of these writings are indicated in the Bibliography.

[2] See *supra*, p. 33.

regions of the Black and Caspian Seas.   England received
practically all her furs from the Northmen traders, who in
turn secured them in Northern Norway and in Russia.   In
the course of time, however, the Norwegian trade in furs
lost ground because of the increasing competition offered by
the Gotlanders, who dealt in Russian furs.

Although the Northmen continued to engage in trade
throughout the viking period, most of them turned to marauding and warfare.   Thus, during the reign of Bectric,
three viking ships came to Dorchester, England.   The Reeve
ordered " them to proceed to the king's town because he
knew not what they were; but they slew him on the spot." [3]
In 793, according to Simeon of Durham, " pagans from the
Northern region came with a naval armament to Britain,
like stinging hornets, and over-ran the country in all direc-
tions, like fierce wolves, plundering, tearing and killing not
only sheep and oxen, but priests and Levites, and choirs of
monks and nuns.   They came . . . to the Church of Lindisfarne, and laid waste with dreadful havoc, trod with un-
hallowed feet the holy places, dug up the altars, and carried
off all the treasures of the holy church.   Some of the breth-
ren they killed; some they carried off in chains; many they
cast out, naked and loaded with insults; some they drowned
in the sea." [4]   In 794 the Northmen appeared at Jarrow,
but this time they were less successful; one of their chieftains
was slain, several of their ships were lost in a storm, and
many vikings were drowned while others who had succeeded
in getting ashore were killed by the Northumbrians.[5]
Cryptic notations in the Annals of Ulster, under 792 and
794, state: " all the coast of Britain ravaged by the foreign-

[3] *Anglo-Saxon Chron.*   Bectric ruled from 787 to 800.

[4] Simeon of Durham, *History of the Kings of England* (transl. by
J. Stevenson, London, 1855), p. 457; *Anglo-Saxon Chron.*

[5] *Anglo-Saxon Chron.*; Simeon of Durham, *op. cit.*, p. 458.

ers," and " the foreigners ravage Fortrenn and distress the Picts."

In 793 the vikings sailed down the Channel, round the south coast and made attacks in Wales. From here they continued to Ireland. In 798 the Isle of Man was visited, and in the following year they appeared in southern France. In the next year the islands along the Frisian coast were raided. Finally, the Northmen found their way to Iona, the island of the Hebrides group on which the foremost sanctuary of the West was located. Hither pilgrims from many lands came every year. Because of its wealth, this monastery was of particular interest to the vikings, and in 802 they swept over the island. In 806 they returned, because in the four-year interval new treasures had been gathered at the church. The chronicles tell us that at this time they also killed sixty-eight clerics who attempted to defend the treasures of the sanctuary.[6] In 807 they rounded the coast of Ireland to plunder Inishmurry, another rich monastery. In 812 a fleet of 120 ships came to Ireland, and in 832 the church of Armagh was plundered three times in one month.[7]

Thus, in the early ninth century, the viking enterprises were being expanded. From piracy and trade the traffic developed into harrying in foreign lands. Marauding became its most important part, and thereby a significant economic function of the North. Viking fleets were cruising to and fro in the Baltic and the North Sea; and in most of the churches the prayer was read: " *A furore Normannorum libera nos Domine!* "

The records suggest that after the attacks upon New Dorchester, Lindisfarne and Jarrow in the years from 787 to 794, there followed a period of four decades during which

---

[6] *Four Masters*, 793, 797, 801 ; Steenstrup, *op. cit.*, vol. ii, p. 13.

[7] *Four Masters*, 807, 808 ; *War of the Gaedhil with the Gaill*, pp. 5, 224 ; *Annals of Ulster*, 832.

no raids were made on English shores.   But in 832 or 834
they began anew.   Numerous towns were attacked, among
them Dorchester, London and York.   Anglia was also invaded.   From here the Northmen began harrying in Mercia,
the adjoining kingdom, and the Mercians were compelled to
pay for peace.   The Northmen observed the terms of the
agreement for about a year.   They gained control of East
Anglia and Wessex.   The marauding activities in these
parts, engaged in chiefly by Danes, lasted down to about
870.[8]

Then followed the struggle that eventuated in the estab-
lishment of the Danelaw or the region that was governed
according to the laws of the Danes (Northmen).   In 871
Alfred the Great ascended the throne of Wessex, but dissension and a defeatist attitude prevailed among the various
kingdoms in England, and the Danes came and went, or
rather remained, practically at will.   During the winter of
871-872, the vikings made their quarters in London and felt
so much at home that Halvdan, their leader, had coins
stamped that bore his name and the London monogram.[9]
Halvdan also successfully demanded tribute from the
Londoners.

In 873 Halvdan began ravaging in Mercia, overthrowing
the ruler in the following year.[10]   Then in 875 the viking
army separated; Halvdan leading one part into Bernicia,
looting monasteries and other wealthy places, while the other
part, under Guthrum, went to Cambridge for the winter.[11]   In
876 Halvdan went to Deira, apparently to settle down, as the
land was portioned out among his followers, who " thence-

[8] *Anglo-Saxon Chron.*, 832-833, 835, 837-838, 840, 845, 851, 853, 860,
865-870.

[9] *London Museum Catalogues, no. 1,* p. 11.

[10] *Anglo-Saxon Chron.*

[11] *Ibid.*

forth were ploughing and providing for themselves." [12]
Guthrum's forces, joined by vikings from Ireland, again
turned to Wessex. Alfred was compelled to buy peace, and
the vikings swore to evacuate Wessex immediately. But
they broke their oath, going to Exeter and ordering their
ships to the mouth of the river Exe.[13] More than 120 ships
were lost, however, in a storm off Swanage. In the meantime Alfred had succeeded in holding the land-force at bay.
As a result of these temporary reverses, the Danes decided
to return to East Anglia, but upon reaching Dorchester, in
Wessex, they encamped. From Dorchester, they made
another attack a few months later upon the surrounding
territory. Halvdan proceeded to take a considerable portion
of Mercia and divided it into five parts, each having a fortified town or " borough " for its center.[14] This marked the
beginning of the " Five Boroughs " and the foundation of
the Danelaw. The viking enterprises in England were entering into their last phase, namely, permanent settlement and
political domination.

In 878 Ebbe, Halvdan's brother, brought a fleet of 23
ships and 840 warriors to re-enforce Halvdan's army.[15]

At this juncture it seemed to be only a matter of time
before the Northmen would control all England. All organized resistance was abandoned. During the winter of 877-
878, Alfred and a small following were roaming about in
the marshes of Somerset. Time and again the Northmen
nearly caught Alfred's band, but finally Alfred found a
haven on the island of Athelney, in the river Parret. Seven

[12] *Ibid.*

[13] " . . . and they swore oaths to him on the holy ring—which never
before would they do to any people—that they should speedily fare from
his kingdom." But "they broke that" and "stole away by night to
Exeter" (*Anglo-Saxon Chron.*, 876).

[14] *Ibid.*

[15] *Ibid.*

days after Easter in 878, he defeated the vikings in the battle of Ethandun in Somerset.   The latter then endeavored to find protection in the port of Chippenham—just east of Bristol—but Alfred surrounded them.   The vikings starved until they asked for peace, and promised under oath never to molest Alfred's kingdom again.   Guthrum, the viking leader, agreed to become a Christian, and sometime later he and thirty of his chieftains were baptized.[16]   He was allowed to retain control over East Anglia, where he apportioned the land among the Northmen.[17]

In the fall of 892, "the great army" arrived from Boulonge in France to England.   There were two fleets in this contingent, one consisting of 250 ships and the other of 80 ships.   In the ensuing struggle, lasting until 896, a number of battles were fought and Alfred generally emerged victorious.[18]   One of the last was the routing in 895 of the Danes from their camp just above London.   The vikings, cut off from the sea, were forced to abandon their ships and to turn overland into Mercia.   In 896 they disbanded; some obtained grants of land in the Danelaw and became peaceful tillers of the soil; others "got themselves ships and fared south over the sea to the Seine," [19] where the viking enterprises at this time were enjoying a period of prosperity.

Alfred's most effective weapon was his fleet.   He also adopted the method of cutting off the enemy's food supply. As a result, from the year 895 to his death in 901, Alfred

---

[16] *Ibid.*, 878.   Upon being baptized, Guthrum received the name Aethelstan.

[17] They "occupied some of the land and apportioned it" (*Anglo-Saxon Chron.*, 880).   It appears that from 879 and for sometime thereafter, the chronology of the Anglo-Saxon Chronicle is one year in advance (Charles Plummer, *Notes to the Anglo-Saxon Chronicle*, Oxford, 1899, p. 95).

[18] *Anglo-Saxon Chron.*

[19] *Ibid.*, 897.

was saved from further attacks upon his kingdom. But the Northmen in East Anglia remained. It was not until 921, when the vikings agreed to join the English in protecting the English shores from invasion, that East Anglia really came under the English crown. Norse laws and institutions prevailed, however, and for decades the Northmen managed their internal affairs independent of English power.

Northumbria was also a lucrative field for the activities of the Northmen. Because of internal dissension, the resistance offered the invaders was negligible. In 875 Halvdan occupied York and the surrounding territory.[20] A long struggle followed between the English and the various bands of Northmen, over the throne of Northumbria. Ragnvald, of the Dublin branch of the house of Ragnar Lodbrok, seized the throne of York, but was soon induced to accept the English king as his overlord. As time went on, other vikings came, generally not from the North directly, but from the Norwegian outposts which by now existed in Ireland, Scotland and the Isle of Man. These Northmen were as a rule less belligerent than their fore-runners and upon arrival generally settled down to peaceful pursuits. But many of them continued to be interested in pillage and plunder and upon occasion gave aid to the Northmen who from time to time attacked southern England.

On the whole Wales and Scotland never afforded very profitable fields of operation for the vikings, since internal strife was less pronounced in these regions. Sporadic raids, however, were made upon Wales. The first known attack on Scotland took place in the year 839, when sixty-five ships which had been harrying in Ireland came to its shores.[21] In 870 there was another major attack, this time out of Ireland. Two viking leaders, Olav and Ivar, besieged Dunbarton for

[20] *Ibid.*, 875.
[21] *War of the Gaedhil with the Gaill*, pp. 13, 236.

four months.   The returns were shipped to Dublin in 200 ships the following year.[22]   Among the prisoners were Britons, Saxons and Scotchmen, indicating that the raiders had covered extensive areas.   Scotland was also drawn into the struggle about political domination which characterized the last century of the viking period.[23]   In 937 the viking leader Olav Cuaran managed to unite the Northmen and the kings of Scotland and Cumberland for an attack upon the English in Northumbria.   Constantine III, the king of the Scots, cast his lot with the Northmen, apparently because he desired the creation of an independent Scandinavian kingdom of Northumbria to serve as a buffer state between Scotland and the English power to the southward.   The plan to create such a kingdom was frustrated, however, in spite of the support given to it by the Celts, who likewise feared the growing Anglo-Saxon power.   Aethelstan, the king of the English, with his army met Olav Cuaran and Constantine at Brunanburh, where one of the bloodiest battles of the entire viking period was fought.[24]   Aethelstan won, but before long another Scandinavian king sat on the throne of Northumbria.   This time, however, the king was Aethelstan's vassal.   Eric Blood-Axe, Norway's former king, who had been ejected from his homeland by his brothers, had gone west on a viking cruise.[25]   Aethelstan offered him Northumbria as a vassalage, provided Eric became a Christian

[22] *Three Fragments*, p. 193; Steenstrup, *op. cit.*, vol. ii, p. 311.

[23] Although never a very remunerative field for marauding, Scotland received many settlers of Scandinavian origin, and "in some parts of the country Norse was still spoken as late as the seventeenth century" (Albert C. Baugh, *A History of the Engl. Language*, New York, 1935, p. 116).

[24] *Anglo-Saxon Chron.*, 937. See also *Egil's Saga*, ch. 52, and Eddison's notes to his transl. of this saga, p. 280.

[25] *Fagrskinna*; *Heimskringla, Saga of Harald Fairhair*; Knut Gjerset, *A History of the Norwegian People*, vol. i, p. 161.

and promised to protect the kingdom from enemies, especially those of the North. These terms were agreeable to Eric. After the death of Aethelstan in 939, Eric's position became less secure, and he found it more convenient to move on to other fields. He continued to be interested in Northumbria, however, and was the chief instigator of the rebellion of 947. In 952 he returned to become earl vassal of Northumbria under Eadred. Two years later he was deposed. He returned to the traditional business on the seas and succeeded in obtaining control over the Hebrides. He also harried in Wales and western England, where he finally was killed by another viking chieftain. Thus the last Scandinavian king had been driven out of Northumbria, " and, though Danish blood and Danish customs remained in undiminished force to distinguish the Danelaw from the rest of the country, by 954 this province had been transformed into a quiescent appanage of the English crown." [26]

But the end of the viking enterprises had not yet come. For almost three decades, or as long as England had strong rulers, the Northmen remained at a distance. But shortly after Edward had ascended the throne in 975, the vikings, finding the opposition weak, renewed their attacks. In 980 seven Danish ships seized Southampton and plundered the city.[27] In the same year Norwegian vikings, presumably from Ireland and the Isle of Man, took Chester and ravaged in the vicinity of the city.[28] During the following two years, Danish vikings swept over southwestern England and entered the Irish Sea.[29] Attacks were also made on several points in Scotland where " seven dozen vikings " were at one time captured and hanged. Shortly afterward, during

[26] Kendrick, *op. cit.*, p. 257.
[27] *Anglo-Saxon Chron.*, 980.
[28] *Florence of Worcester*, 980.
[29] *Anglo-Saxon Chron.*, 982.

the very Christmas night, Northmen raided Iona monastery and killed the abbot and fifteen of the monks,[30] Later they visited Wales and Devonshire.[31] About a decade later, in 991, a fleet consisting of 93 ships sailed up the Thames to plunder the shores of that river, Suffolk and Essex.[32] One of the viking chieftains is said to have been brought up in Gardarik; [33] a tradition which suggests that some of these warriors came from the Swedish settlements in Russia. At this time there was also considerable plundering in Sandwich and in Ipswich.[34] At Maldon the vikings won a decisive victory over the English. This battle is of special interest because of the curious sidelights that the preliminaries throw upon the method of warfare at the time. The vikings were encamped on the island of Northey,[35] in the estuary of the Blackwater, and the English had drawn up on the river bank opposite the vikings. The Northmen presented their ultimatum, which the famous epic " *The Battle of Maldon* " depicts as follows:

The viking's herald stood on shore, and threateningly and loud
He gave the earl upon the bank the seafolk's message proud.
We need not spoil each other's lives if ye make fast aright
A peace with us; if thou agree, thou, here the most of might,
Thy folk to ransom, and to give the seamen what shall be
Right in their eyes, and take out peace, make peace with told
        money,
We'll haste to ship, we'll keep that peace, and go upon the sea.

[30] *Four Masters*, 985; *Chronicon Scotorum*, 984.

[31] *Anglo-Saxon Chron.*, 981 ; *Florence of Worcester*, 981.

[32] *Anglo-Saxon Chron.*

[33] *Gardarik* or *Gardariki* was the Old Norse name for Russia.

[34] *Anglo-Saxon Chron.*, 991.

[35] That the battle took place close to the island of Northey has been established by E. D. Laborde (" The Site of the Battle of Maldon," *Eng. Hist. Review*, vol. 40, pp. 161-173).

But in the midst of their negotiations the tide arrived and submerged the causeway. As the vikings thus were unable to get across to commence battle, they suggested that the English permit them to cross unmolested. There seems to have been nothing unorthodox in this request, for the English readily complied. When the Northmen finally had crossed, the two armies lined up for battle. Brithnoth, the East Anglican leader, was slain; some of his men managed to flee, but a large number met their death on the battlefield. Thereupon the English had to buy peace for 10,000 pounds and to guarantee the rations for the viking army during its sojourn in England. This was the first Danegeld or tribute exacted by the Danes (Northmen) in England.[36] Others were to follow.

The vikings went to East Anglia. In the meantime Aethelred gathered a fleet in London which he sent against them, but a treacherous alderman of London warned the Northmen so that they were able to get away, losing only one ship.[37] In 993 the vikings plundered Bamborough, and in the following year Olav of Norway appeared in London with 94 ships.[38] After an unsuccessful attack on the city, he proceeded to ravage southeastern England.[39] Again peace had to be bought, this time for a price of 16,000 pounds and free maintenance for the viking army during the following winter. The maintenance " was defrayed by Wessex,

[36] *Anglo-Saxon.* "A tribute was given to the Danes for the first time; ten thousand pounds being paid to them in consideration of their desisting from the constant pillage, burnings and homicides which they practiced all along the coast, and of their concluding a settled peace" (*Florence of Worcester*, 891). It is believed, however, that Danegeld was promised if not actually paid before this date or as early as 865, as recorded in the *Anglo-Saxon Chronicle. Cf.* Charles Plummer, *op. cit.,* p. 175.

[37] *Anglo-Saxon Chron.*, 992.

[38] *Florence of Worcester*, 993, 994.

[39] *Ibid.*, 994.

but the tribute was levied throughout England." A part of the viking army under the leadership of Olav Tryggvason returned to Norway in 995 to secure the throne of that country from Hakon Jarl. Some of the remaining vikings went pillaging in northwestern Germany and Schleswig.

In the year 1002 " the king and his witan decreed that 24,000 pounds should be paid to the fleet on condition that they should cease from their evil-doings." [40] A few years later, in 1007, 3,000 pounds were collected in Kent by Thorkel, the alleged Jomsviking, who thereupon established himself on Man and, in spite of promises to the contrary, proceeded to ravage in Sussex, Hampshire and Berkshire. Later Essex was also invaded. In 1010 the vikings spent three months harrying in East Anglia, the colony of their forefathers, in which the population still was half Danish and where Danish law still prevailed. Thetford, Cambridge, Northampton and other towns were burned. [41] The success of the Northmen in these campaigns was due not entirely to their strength and clever strategy, but also to treason and mismanagement on the part of the English. The *Anglo-Saxon Chronicle* states that " all these calamities fell upon us through ill-counsel, because tribute was not offered to them at the right time, nor yet were they resisted; but, when they had done most evil, then was peace made with them. And

[40] *Anglo-Saxon Chron.*

[41] " The Northmen had then overrun 1. East Anglia, 2. Essex, 3. Middlesex, 4. Oxfordshire, 5. Cambridgeshire, 6. Hertfordshire, 7. Buckinghamshire, 8. Bedfordshire, and 9. half Huntingdonshire and 10. much in Northamptonshire; and to the south of the Thames, all Kent and Sussex and Hastings and Hampshire and much in Wiltshire " (*Anglo-Saxon Chron.*, 1011).

Florence of Worcester (*Anno* 1011), reveals that during the siege of Canterbury in Kent " some of the towns-people were put to death at the sword, others perished in the flames . . . and some were hung by their private parts till they expired."

notwithstanding all this peace and tribute, they fared everywhere in troops, harried our people, captured and slew them."

Svein, the king of Denmark, heard of the success of Thorkel and decided to participate in the enterprises. In July of 1010 he set sail for England. Upon arrival he was accepted as the overlord of Northumbria and Danish Mercia. Gradually he managed to obtain a foothold also west of Watling Street and, in the end, became the actual ruler of all England, the English king having fled to Normandy.[42] To be the ruler meant primarily to have the right to exact tributes; even London had to make payments to him.

When Svein died in 1014, two of his sons, Harald—at home in Denmark—and Cnut, who had been chosen to head the army in England, began to quarrel about the succession to the throne of England. The English realized that now there might be an opportunity for them to regain their independence. Aethelred, the English king, was asked to return from Normandy to lead the English in their fight for freedom. When Cnut heard of this, he at once went to Denmark to obtain additional warriors and equipment. In the meantime Aethelred was making his preparations. He paid 21,000 pounds to Thorkel and Olav, presumably on the condition that they would aid him against Cnut.[43] This investment proved to be a very poor one, because Thorkel soon set sail for Denmark to place himself under Cnut, and Olav undertook an independent venture in the traditional viking manner to the shores of the Continent.

In the battles which followed Cnut's arrival, the Northmen generally were victorious. Aethelred died in 1016, in the midst of this struggle, and was succeeded by his son Edmund, later called Edmund Ironside. Edmund had the

[42] " The king went over sea and was there until the fortunate occasion when Swagen [Svein] was dead " (*Anglo-Saxon Chron.*, 1013).

[43] *Anglo-Saxon Chron.*, 1014.

upper hand until Eadric, the Duke of West Mercia, lost the cause by his flight from the battlefield at Ashington in Essex.[44] Cnut pursued the retreating Edmund, who was forced to seek terms. It was agreed that Edmund was to hold Wessex while Cnut got Mercia and the Danelaw. London was granted peace upon the payment of 11,000 pounds to Cnut.[45] When Edmund Ironside in November, 1016, suddenly died, the nobles of Wessex turned to Cnut, avowedly the strongest leader available, and chose him as their king. In the capacity of sovereign of all England, Cnut found it much easier to exact the coveted tribute; in addition to the above payment of the Londoners, he succeeded in 1018 in collecting the enormous amount of 72,000 pounds, ostensibly as a charge for the " protection " that his Danish mercenaries afforded England.[46]

The ultimate phase of the viking enterprises had become firmly established in England. The Northmen had become supreme, and one of their own number sat on the throne. But this also marked the beginning of the end of viking domination in this region. As rulers the Northmen had to protect the country from the outside. In this they were successful, with the result that other vikings from the North found it increasingly difficult to make marauding profitable in England. The last spurt of the viking drive appeared in 1066, when Tostig sought help in Norway to oust his brother from the throne of England, and a Norwegian fleet went to England with a large army.[47] This army was defeated at Stamford Bridge. A few weeks later William the Con-

---

[44] About Eadric the *Anglo-Saxon Chronicle* states: " He betrayed his king and lord and the whole English nation, and Cnut won the victory, and gained all England for himself."

[45] *Anglo-Saxon Chron.*, 1018; *cf. Florence of Worcester*, 1018; F. W. Maitland, *Domesday and Beyond* (Cambridge, 1897), p. 3.

[46] " for the pay of the Danish army " (*Florence of Worcester*, 1018).

[47] *Anglo-Saxon Chron.*

queror arrived in England, and in the memorable battle of Hastings, Harald Godwinsson, the last of the Anglo-Scandinavian kings, fell. The exact amounts collected by the vikings in the insular regions of northwestern Europe cannot be ascertained. The figure for England is generally considered to be about 220,000 pounds, the total of some ten payments, beginning in the year 891. It is clear, however, that Danegeld was promised, if not actually paid, as early as 865, as recorded in the *Anglo-Saxon Chronicle*. The same source states that prior to 991 the Danegeld was 10,000 pounds, but it may well have been considerably higher.[48] Up to 1012 the Danegeld in England was paid as the purchase price of peace; after that date, until 1051, when the fleet of the mercenaries was dismissed by Edward the Confessor, it was paid as a stipend to the Danish mercenaries in the service of the English.[49] The amounts paid in order to secure peace were as follows: 16,000 pounds in 884, 24,000 in 1002, 30,000 in 1007 and 3,000 (from East Kent) in 1009. The sum of 21,000 pounds was raised in 1014, and in 1018, after having been crowned, Cnut took 83,000 pounds, 11,000 of which was handed over by the Londoners. In 1040 Harthacnut exacted 21,099 pounds, besides a sum of 11,048 pounds that was paid for thirty-two ships.[50] In addition there were several war-taxes levied by Danish rulers, the amounts of which are unknown. The sums received as ransom are likewise imposssible to determine.

Imposing though they are, these figures by no means tell the whole story of the profits made by the vikings in England. If they were calculable, the aggregate takings in the

[48] *Cf.* Charles Plummer, *op. cit.*, p. 175.

[49] Einar Joranson, *Danegeld in France*, in *Augustana College Library Publications, no. 10* (Rock Island, 1923), p. 15.

[50] Maitland, *op. cit.*, p. 3.

regular routine of pillage over more than two centuries would doubtless show returns several times larger than those indicated by the cash payments.   In addition there were the profits derived from trade, as many Northmen were also traders, some regularly and some when marauding was less profitable.

The trade between the North and England during the period reached its greatest height from 1017 to 1042.[51] Just outside the city wall in London, Danish seafarers had their own church (*ecclesia sancta Danorum*), the site of which is still called St. Clements Danes in the Strand.   The Northmen enjoyed many privileges in London; they could remain in the city throughout the year.   They had their own gild house and stood to all appearances on an equal footing with the London merchants.   But their trading activities in England were by no means confined to London.   They had access to all fairs and markets in England.   Most of the commercially important cities in England were either founded or settled by Northmen, large numbers of whom came as warrior vikings.   One of the more prominent of these cities was Grimsby.   Here, as shown by a document still extant in the Public Record Office in London, the Northmen were given special customs privileges as late as during the reign of Henric I (1100-1135).[52]   All the English place-names ending in -by, of which there are 1,373,[53] show Scandinavian influence, the " by " being the Scandinavian term for town.   The contributions made to English shipping by the people of the Scandinavian North were especially large, and it can hardly be considered a mere coincidence that the

[51] W. Vogel, *Nordische Seefahrten im früheren Mittelalter*, p. 9.

[52] *Flateyjarbok, ii*, 440; Charles Gross, *The Gild Merchant* (Oxford, 1890), vol. iii, p. 377.

[53] J. A. A. Worsaae, *An Account of the Danes and Norwegians in Scotland and Ireland* (London, 1852), p. 71.

towns in which the Scandinavian element was preponderant became the foremost shipping towns in all England in the Middle Ages. The viking expeditions to Ireland began approximately at the same time as those to England. The first recorded attack took place in 795, when the Northmen plundered the church on Lambay Island, just north of Dublin.[54] After a twelve-year respite, there followed a period of occasional attacks which lasted almost a quarter of a century. Then, already in 830, the final phase of the viking enterprises was inaugurated in Ireland. Instead of making sporadic attacks, some of the marauders, in this case mostly Norwegians, began to settle in Ulster.[55] Thus we find that colonization in Ireland began almost half a century earlier than it did in England. In 832, Turgeis, a Norwegian chieftain, arrived in Ulster and made himself king over his countrymen there.[56] The coming of Turgeis coincided with the plundering of the Irish monasteries undertaken by Feidlimid, the priest-king of Munster, who aspired to become the spiritual head of all Ireland. The Irish revolted at the outrages of Feidlimid, who in cruelty managed to " outviking " the vikings, and this naturally made the task of Turgeis considerably easier. He succeeded in gaining control over the revenues of the

[54] Zimmer's contention that the entry under the year 617 in the *Annals of Ulster* which reads : " the devastation of Tory Island by a marine fleet," refers to a viking attack has not been substantiated (*Sitzungsberichte der Kgl. Preus. Akademie der Wissenschaften*, Bd. i, pp. 279 *et seq.*). It is more likely that this attack was made by others than Northmen. Miss Walsh believes that the attack of 617 was " due to Saxon and Pictish raiders rather than Norsemen" (*Scandinavian Relations with Ireland during the Viking Period*, Dublin, 1932, p. 1).

[55] *Four Masters*, 835; Kendick, *op. cit.*, pp. 275-276.

[56] The saga-description of Thorgils (*Heimskringla, Saga of Harald Fairhar*, 34) bears a close resemblance to the Irish accounts of Turgeis (Old Norse, *Thorgest*). See Walsh, *op. cit.*, p. 2.

rich monastery of Armaugh, the ecclesiastical center of all Ireland.

Reports of the success of Turgeis had reached Scandinavia, and soon he had a large number of competitors. The latter established themselves along the coast in the South and toward the East. In time their settlements grew and became the towns of Amagassan, Dublin, Wexford, Waterford and Limerick. Using these centers as bases for their operations, they ravaged the surrounding territory.[57] The Irish gradually gained the upper hand, chiefly because of lack of efficient leadership among the vikings.

When the Northmen in England, most of whom were Danes, learned that the Norwegians were having difficulties with the Irish, they also began to take an interest in this region. In 849 they appeared, 140 ships strong, and a fierce struggle between the Dubhgaill (Danes) and the Finngaill (Norwegians) occurred.[58] In 851 the Danes defeated the Norwegians in the great three-days' naval battle on Carlingford Loch. The Norwegians lost heavily.[59] After the battle, the chronicler tells us, Maelsaecklainn, the Irish chief ruler, sent messengers to the Danes. They found the Danes cooking food in large kettles placed over the bodies of fallen Norwegians, the corpses of whom had been piled up into heaps. The corpses which were impaled by the spits used for roasting the meat were burned by the fires until they burst open. When the Irish messengers expressed their wonder at such behavior, the Danes replied: " They would have done the same thing to us, had they had a chance."

---

[57] *Four Masters*, 840-843; *Chronicon Scotorum*, 841.

[58] *Chronicon Scotorum*, 849.

[59] The records indicate 5,000 men, but such a large number may be considered questionable. See *Three Fragments*, pp. 119 *et seq.*; *War of the Gaedhil with the Gaill*, p. 19; *Four Masters*, 850; and *Chronicon Scotorum*, 851, 852.

The Danes then gave to the Irish envoys a large chest of gold and silver for St. Patrick. " The Danes were a people possessed of a sort of piety," the chronicler avers. " They could for a time give up both food and women for the sake of piety."[60] Later in the same year, the Irish attacked the weakened Norwegians, who are reputed to have lost 500 men.[61]

In the years following the battle on Carlingford Loch, the Norwegians, reenforced from their homeland, regained some of their former power and prestige. Among others, Olav the White, a great and experienced viking, came with a large fleet; and not only the Norwegians, but also the Danes and the Irish, were forced to pay him tribute.[62] Many of the Danes left Dublin, however, to go harrying in Britain, and Dublin virtually became a Norwegian town.[63] By 870 it was " the acknowledged headquarters of viking activity, not only in Erin, but in all Western waters."[64] During the sixties and, to a lesser extent, also in the seventies, sporadic viking attacks were directed against various points both in Ireland and elsewhere.[65] When there was no more to be had from the living, they turned to the dead, and many graves of the wealthy men of the past were thoroughly ransacked.[66] As time elapsed, however, fewer and fewer con-

[60] *Three Fragments*, pp. 123 *et seq.*

[61] *Four Masters*, 850; *Chronicon Scotorum*, 852; *Three Fragments*, p. 125; *War of the Gaedhil with the Gaill*, p. 21.

[62] *Four Masters*, 851; *Chronicon Scotorum*, 853.

[63] See L. J. Vogt, *Dublin som norsk By* (Oslo, 1896).

[64] T. D. Kendrick, *op. cit.*, p. 280.

[65] See Steenstrup, *op. cit.*, vol. ii, pp. 129-141.

[66] *Four Masters*, 861; *Three Fragments*, p. 153. It is doubtless activities of this nature that the following saga account describes. " Lief went on voyages of plunder to the West; he harried in Ireland and found there a large dungeon. He entered and found it very dark; only the sword, which a man held in his hand, shone. Lief killed the man and

tingents of Norwegians arrived from the home country, with the result that the Norwegian settlement in Ireland began to dwindle in strength and importance. Through intermarriage with the Irish, many of the Northmen gradually became " Irish-conscious." [67]   Not a few Northmen in Ireland moved to the smaller islands to the North; a number of families went to Iceland.[68]   Dissension among the remaining Norwegians further weakened them, and less than a generation later, in 902, the Irish had no difficulty in taking Dublin.

But in the second decade of the tenth century, there began a period of renewed activity in Ireland.   In 913 a large fleet came to Waterford to ravage in Munster and Leinster. In 916 another fleet landed at Cenn Fuaid in Leinster.   The two fleets having united their forces, Dublin was taken shortly thereafter.   Since their operations proved very successful, the Gaill, i. e., the " foreigners," were induced to exert still greater efforts.   By 920 Scandinavian power in Ireland was at its height; and from 920 to 950, through its connection with the Scandinavian kingdom of Northumbria, Dublin gained consistently in importance.[69]   But the struggle between the Irish and the Gaill continued, although many Northmen had begun to adjust themselves to their new environment.[70]   When the vikings were not harrying on other

took the sword and much goods from him.   From then on he was called Sword-Lief.   Sword-Lief harried widely in Ireland and took much goods and ten slaves " (*Landnámabók*, i, 5; Steenstrup, *op. cit.*, vol. ii, p. 142).

[67] For references to such marriages see *Landnámabók*, i, 1; iii, 10, 12; v, 8, 13.   One of the daughters of the Irish king Cearbhall of Ossory (d. 887) was the wife of Eyvind the Easterner "who settled down in Ireland and had charge of Kjarval's defenses." *Cf. Grettis Saga*, ch. 3.

[68] *Landnámabók*, i, 5, 10, 14, 15; ii, 22, 24, 26; iii, 12; iv, 11; v, 13.

[69] A. Walsh, *op. cit.*, p. 5.

[70] Many of them had accepted Christianity, at least nominally, and had, through trade and barter, established peaceful contacts with the Irish.

shores, they were generally fighting the Irish at home. The most sanguine of the combats was the battle of Sulcoit in Tipperary, in which the vikings were defeated. Every captured viking who was fit for war was killed; and the others were enslaved.[71] In spite of this set-back, they regained some of their former strength and were not decisively beaten until 1014, in the famous battle of Clontarf. Although weakened in power, the Northmen remained in possession of Dublin till the following year, and some of their settlements in Ireland persisted until the English conquered the island a century and a half later. After the battle of Clontarf, smaller contingents of Northmen arrived at irregular intervals from overseas, and the settlers of Nordic blood remained to contribute, by their trade, wealth and talent for organization, to the Irish commonwealth.[72]

Ireland's commercially important towns owe a great deal to the Northmen, as the first Irish trade with the outside world seems to have been begun by Norwegians and Danes residing in Ireland. Dublin, Limerick, Cork and Waterford were the chief centers.[73] From these towns the ships of the Northmen sailed across the Irish Sea to Scotland and England, notably to Bristol, in those days an important center of the slave trade. The Northmen also sailed to Noirmoutiers, Nantes and Bordeaux, where they obtained wine, arms and products of the Levant. From Limerick they sailed to Spain for leather, cloth and clothing. From Dublin and the Hebrides they also went to the various parts of their homelands and to Russia.

Toward the close of the twelfth century many of the characteristics of the Northmen in Ireland had disappeared, but marked influences in language and nationality remained

[71] *War of the Gaedhil with the Gaill*, p. 81.
[72] T. D. Kendrick, *op. cit.*, p. 298.
[73] See A. Walsh, *op. cit.*, pp. 22-27.

far into the fourteenth century and perhaps longer. This particular injection of Northern blood was completed and, as has been the case elsewhere where they have gone, the Northmen were soon merged with the people among whom they lived. But " traces of the Scandinavian occupation still remain," however, "in the place-names on the coast, especially in the districts surrounding the seaport towns." The very name Ireland (Old Norse *Iraland*) " is Scandinavian in form and replaced the old Irish word *Eriu* during the viking period." [74]

The Northmen also found their way to the Hebrides, Man, Shetland and the Orkneys.[75]   Reference has already been made to the earlier attacks upon the wealthy monastery on Iona, one of the Hebrides.   In 885 a third attack was made upon this monastery, which had been rebuilt on a new site.   Having been informed of the approach of the viking fleet, the monks hurried to bury the treasure shrine, and when the abbot, Blotmac mac Flainn, refused to reveal the hiding place, he was killed at the altar.[76]   Men from the North, chiefly Norwegians, had settled in the islands off Scotland at the very beginning of the viking age, or before 820.   Others came later as a result of the oftentime high-handed policies of King Harald Fairhair during the period of unification of Norway.[77]   Using these islands as bases of operation, they pillaged far and wide, even in Norway.[78] In fact, all the island colonies were at one time or another under viking domination, and both social and linguistic in-

[74] *Ibid.*, pp. 27, 28.

[75] *Three Fragments*, p. 159; *Heimskringla, Saga of Harald Fairhair*, 27.

[76] See Steenstrup, *op. cit.*, vol. ii, pp. 35-36.

[77] " The out-countries of Iceland and the Faroe Islands were discovered and peopled " (*Heimskringla, Saga of Harald Fairhair*, 20).

[78] " In winter they were in the Orkney Islands and Hebrides; but marauded in summer in Norway, and did great damage " (*ibid.*).

fluences of the North were long discernible in these places. Some are still noticeable, such as place-names and certain expressions in the prevailing dialects. The fact that no really large estates exist on Man, while they abound in England and Scotland, has been ascribed to Scandinavian influences brought down from the time that the Northmen ruled the island.[79]

Sometime after 860, Naddod, a Norwegian, and Gardar, a Swede, came to Iceland, but this island had been discovered somewhat earlier by Irish monks.[80] About 873 there began a wave of migration to Iceland which lasted five or six decades. The great majority of the settlers came from Norway directly, but among them were also many Northmen and some Celts from Ireland and the British Isles. Of those listed in the *Landnámabók* (Book of Settlement) 84 per cent came from Norway, 3 per cent from Sweden, and 12.6 per cent from the British Isles.[81] The settling of Iceland was not really a part of the viking business proper, as the motive was not " to get rich quick " through plunder, but land-hunger and a desire to escape from political suppression at home.[82] Many vikings, both leaders and ordinary participants in the viking activities, hailed from Iceland.

[79] Bugge, *Vesterlandenes indflydelse*, etc., p. 91 ; Francis Palgrave, *The Rise and Progress of the English Commonwealth* (Cambridge, 1921), pt. i, pp. 77, 98.

[80] Nansen, *op. cit.*, vol. i, p. 252; H. Hermannsson, *Islandica*, vol. xx (1930), pp. 1-2.

[81] *Ibid.*, p. 8.

[82] *Cf. ibid.*, pp. 6-9. " Iceland was populated in the days of Harald Fairhair ; because the people of Norway would not tolerate the suppression that the king subjected them to, that is, those who were of high-born families and of independent mind and had power and wealth. They thought it better to leave their land and property than to be victims of injustice, either at the hands of the king or any other man " (*Hardar Saga Grimkellssonar*).

Other results of the viking enterprises were the settling of the Faroe Islands and Greenland, and the discovery of Vinland or North America.

In the course of two centuries and a half, the viking activities in the insular parts of Northwestern Europe grew from sporadic raids to politico-military operations and colonization. A similar development took place in the continental phase of the viking aggression.

CHAPTER VIII

OPERATIONS ON THE WESTERN SHORES OF CONTINENTAL EUROPE

THE western shores of Continental Europe also afforded lucrative fields for the vikings. In 806 and 810 the Danes, under King Godfred, launched attacks upon the coast of Aquitaine and in Frisia. In 812 and 813, the Danes had again been plundering in Frisia, and by 820 they had taken possession of the island of Noirmoutier at the mouth of the Loire.[1] There they remained for a long time, making this strategically located island the base of their operations and also their headquarters in the winter, when they were not plundering. The successors to Charlemagne were weak rulers, and the Danes made the most of the situation. Frisia had to endure many attacks; local tributes were exacted in the years 810, 836, 837, 846 and 852.[2] Dorstad was raided at least four times and Antwerp once.[3]

Encouraged by the dissension among the sons of Louis the Pious, the vikings in 841 sailed up the Seine. Rouen was burned, as was the cloister Jumieges.[4] The monastery

[1] Bouquet, *Historiens*, vol. vi, p. 563. Quoted in Steenstrup, *op. cit.*, vol. ii, p. 38.

[2] Joranson, *op. cit.*, pp. 237, 16. For comments on the justification of applying the term Danegeld to the tributes obtained in other countries than England, see *ibid.*, pp. 23-24.

[3] *Annales Fuldenses*; *Annales Xantenses*.

[4] Ordericus Vitalis, *The Ecclesiastical History of England and Normandy* (transl. by T. Forester, London, 1853), vol. i.

of St. Vandrille paid over six pounds, presumably because that was all the money the monastery could raise.[5] The monks of St. Denis cloister ransomed sixty-eight prisoners for twenty-six pounds.[6] In the next year other vikings appeared, this time from England, where they had been engaged in pillage, and raided Quentovic, at the mouth of the Canche. In 843 one of the contenders for the region which approximately corresponds to what is now known as the Department of Nantes, sought the support of the vikings. Promptly the Northmen appeared, and on Midsummer's Day of that year they sacked the city of Nantes.[7] In the next year they were active along the shores of the Geronne. Later they went south to Portugal and Spain. Although more than seventy ships were burned and a large number of Northmen drowned in their first encounter with the people to the south of the Pyrenees, re-enforcements soon arrived from Noirmoutier, so that they still had a formidable fleet when they began their attack on Lisbon. An Arab writer states that "the sea seemed covered with dark red birds." [8] After a month of fighting in Lisbon, they went to Cadiz and advanced to Seville. After losing many men, they started back for the Hebrides and Ireland, plundering as they went along and not forgetting to pay another visit to Lisbon.[9]

As a rule the vikings possessed considerable information about the terrain of the raided regions, a fact which presupposes a fairly well developed system of reconnoitering.[10] They appear to have been especially well informed of the conditions within the Carolingian Empire. As soon as there

[5] *Chronicon Fontanellense*, 841.

[6] *Ibid.*; *Annales Bertiniani*, 841.

[7] *Chronicon Fontanellense*.

[8] Steenstrup, *op. cit.*, vol. ii, p. 290.

[9] *Ibid.*, pp. 291 *et seq.*

[10] Steenstrup, *op. cit.*, vol. i, p. 364.

were any signs of dissension or other weaknesses, the vikings would suddenly arrive. Thus, in 845, six hundred Danish ships sailed up the Elbe. Hamburg, the easternmost outpost of the Carolingian Empire, was captured and practically destroyed.[11] On the day before Easter of the same year, one hundred and twenty ships appeared on the Seine and besieged Paris. Charles the Bald, although possessing a superior army, offered the invaders a sum of money to depart. After having plundered Paris, the vikings received 7,000 pounds of silver and sailed for home, promising that they henceforth would leave the Carolingians in peace.[12]

In 846 the Northmen again came to Frisia to raid and destroy. Dorstad and other cities were burned. In the following year they returned to the same region. As the spoils were large, they appeared also in the year after that, demanding new tribute.[13] An agreement was made with the Frisians whereby this particular contingent of vikings, in return for tribute, not only promised to leave the Frisians alone but also guaranteed to protect them against the attacks of other vikings. Frisia was left in relative peace for several years, but in the meantime the vikings were active in Flanders and Saxony, to which the agreement did not apply.[14]

During the following decade the dominion of the West Franks, a part of the Carolingian Empire, attracted the vikings the most,[15] but the Northmen harried also in many other parts of France and in the Netherlands; they came up the rivers Seine, Loire, Cher, Garonne, Dordognes, Scheldt,

[11] *Annales Fuldenses.*
[12] *Annales Bertiniani*; *Chronicon Fontanellense*; *Annales Fuldenses.*
[13] *Annales Bertiniani*, 846, 847; *Annales Xantenses*, 846, 847.
[14] See *Annales Bertiniani*, 850; Steenstrup, *op. cit.*, vol. i, p. 160.
[15] *Annales Fuldenses.*

Maas and the Rhine.[16]   Ghent and Bordeaux were burned, and many other cities plundered.   A tribute of unknown amount was collected by Sydroc and Godfred, who spent the winter of 852-853 just beyond Rouen.[17]   The campaigns in Brittany proved so profitable that " envious countrymen " of the marauders appeared to share the spoils of the first-comers.[18]   Sydroc, the leader of the second advance, surrounded the vikings who had harassed the Bretons, and invited the Count of Brittany to join him in an attack upon them.   The Count promptly accepted, but Sydroc soon sold out to the enemy for half of the treasures that these vikings had gathered in their earlier campaigns.   Thereupon the first-comers again turned to Brittany and Aquitaine in order to recoup their loss.[19]   Mention is also made of the capture of a Breton chieftain who was later released upon the payment of a considerable ransom in gold.[20]   Charles the Bald tried unsuccessfully to get rid of these insatiable marauders.   At times he fought them and won a battle now and then; but more often he was defeated.   Generally he attempted to buy them off; however, when one army had been paid and had gone elsewhere to harry, a new one appeared with new demands.   Their harrying was by no means confined to the coastline; cities like Tours, Blois and Orleans also became their victims.[21]

In 858 a contingent of vikings captured two half-brothers, Louis and Ganzelin, abbots of St. Denis and Glanfeuil re-

[16] *Annales Bertiniani*, 848, 849, 852, 853, 856, 857, 858, 859; *Chronicon Fontanellense*, 862; *Annales Fuldenses*, 852.

[17] Joranson, *op. cit.*, pp. 40-43.

[18] Steenstrup, *op. cit.*, vol. ii, p. 251.

[19] *Annales Bertiniani*, 855.

[20] Certain monks surrendered a goblet and a platter of gold.   The chieftain reimbursed the monks with land (Steenstrup, *op. cit.*, vol. ii, p. 253).

[21] *Annales Fuldenses*, 853; *Annales Xantenses*, 854.

spectively. Louis, a grandson of Charlemagne and a high-ranking official at the court of Charles the Bald, proved an especially good catch. His release was effected upon the payment of no less than 688 pounds of gold and 3,250 pounds of silver. Since this enormous amount could not be raised by the monastery of St. Denis alone, " Charles the Bald found it necessary to empty the treasuries of many churches in his kingdom." Large contributions were also made by " the king and all the bishops, abbots, counts, and other magnates." Abbot Ganzalin's ransom, an unknown amount, was paid by the Church of Rheims, of which he had formerly been a priest.[22]

While Louis the German and Charles the Bald were fighting over the succession to Lothar, the vikings made the most of the situation. The peasants, who more than others were the victims, rebelled, and those of the hamlets and country-sides between the Loire and the Seine tried hard to repel the Northmen. But they were unsuccessful, as the nobles turned against the peasants and helped to disperse the army of farmers who, on their own initiative and without the aid of their recognized leaders, had taken a stand against the intruders from the North.[23]

If the vikings were in a position to exact tribute, it did not matter so very much who the victim was. In the summer of 859 two contingents of vikings were operating in Francia; one was infesting the basin of the Seine and the other that of the Somme. Early in 860 Welland, the leader of the vikings at the Somme, offered to drive out the vikings at the Seine for 3,000 pounds of silver.[24] The offer was accepted, but when Charles the Bald was unable to raise the funds, the Somme vikings grew impatient, demanded host-

[22] Joranson, *op. cit.*, p. 188.
[23] *Annales Bertiniani*, 859.
[24] *Ibid.*, 860.

ages, and went harrying in England and Flanders. The fact
that they asked for hostages may be construed to mean that
they intended to hold Charles to his contract, although will-
ing to give him more time in which to procure the sum
agreed upon.[25]   Welland returned the following year, ready
to carry out his part of the agreement and to collect the
stipulated amount. But while in England, Welland had
taken pains to strengthen his army, with the result that he
now demanded and received 5,000 pounds of silver instead
of the 3,000 originally agreed upon. In addition he was
furnished with large quantities of grain and cattle.[26] The
campaign against the vikings at the Seine was equally profitable to Welland and his men. At Oscellus he forced them
to capitulate and to hand over 6,000 pounds in silver and
gold. This incident throws considerable light upon the
profitableness of the viking enterprises, as this amount of
6,000 pounds of silver was not necessarily all the " takings "
of the Somme vikings in their campaigns in the heart of the
rich West Frankish kingdom.[27]

But this clash between viking and viking had no lasting
effects. Before long both these groups of Northmen were
again harrying side by side. They were so effective in their
operations that the ever-reluctant Charles the Bald finally
had no other choice but to resist them by force of arms. He
succeeded in expelling the Seine vikings and compelled them
to release their prisoners. These Northmen then turned
toward Brittany, where they agreed to become mercenaries
under Robert, Duke of Neustria, in the latter's war against
Duke Solomon of Brittany. For their services the vikings
collected 6,000 pounds of silver.[28]

[25] Joranson, *op. cit.*, p. 51.

[26] *Annales Bertiniani*, 861 ; Joranson, *op. cit.*, p. 52.

[27] *Anglo-Saxon Chron.*, 860; *Cf.* Joranson, *op. cit.*, p. 55, note 63.

[28] *Annales Bertiniani*, 862.

In the middle of the ninth century, the vikings found their way to the shores of the Mediterranean. Mention has already been made of the voyage to Lisbon and Seville in 844. In 859 Northmen appeared in Galicia and were defeated by its governor. Then they went south, again to be repelled at the mouth of the river Guadalquivir. Thereupon they sailed through the Strait of Gibraltar into the Mediterranean, stopping off at Algeciras to burn its mosque. Next they went to Nekor, the present-day Mezemma, on the coast of Morocco. In a hard-fought battle with the Moors, they were victorious, and captured, in addition to much booty, two Moorish princesses and many slaves. The princesses were promptly bought back by the Moors, while the slaves were brought to Ireland, where they were " dubbed " *Fir gorm* or " blue men." [29] Thereupon the vikings in Morocco separated into two groups. One fleet returned through the Strait of Gibraltar and thence to Ireland, while the other harried the shores of Mercia in Mediterranean Spain. Thence the latter vikings went to the Balearic Islands, later to establish winter quarters on the island of Camargue, at the mouth of the Rhone. After a profitable trip up the Rhone, they turned homeward through the Strait of Gibraltar, visiting on their way the Pamplonians in the province of Navarre, who were permitted to purchase immunity for 90,000 denares. [30] In 862 they arrived in Brittany, and intense warfare followed in this province as well as in Anjou and the vicinity. Many of them served as mercenaries in the struggle between Robert of Neustria and Solomon of Brittany.

[29] The Old Norse " *blaumenn* " may be translated " dark men ". In the North, Africa was referred to as *Blauland*. These " dark men " long remained in Ireland and are mentioned in the Irish chronicles. See *Three Fragments*, pp. 162-163; Steenstrup, *op. cit.*, vol. ii, p. 297.

[30] Steenstrup, *op. cit.*, vol. ii, pp. 296-302.

In 863 the Northmen turned to Aquitaine for a few years of plunder. In 865 they went up the Seine to Pitres and sacked Orleans, Portiers and other towns.[31] In January of 866 they met Charles the Bald, who by this time had succeeded in raising an army, at Melun, on the other side of Paris. When the vikings began to attack the Franks, the latter fled without striking a blow.[32] After this fiasco, Charles was compelled to pay for peace. This time the charge was 4,000 pounds of silver " according to the Northmen's weight ", and a quantity of wine.[33] Having received the tribute, the vikings put to sea, and, for a whole decade, the Seine region was free from their depredations.

In the region along the Loire, the vikings were ineffectively opposed by Charles the Bald and Solomon of Brittany. The latter made peace with the viking leader Hastein and recognized his right to remain unmolested on the lower Loire. But with the approach of spring in 872, Hastein suddenly took to his ships and rowed up to Angers, whose population fled to the interior. Instead of making a raid and then moving on, as was generally the viking custom, Hastein remained. The city, situated on a high cliff-island in the river Mayenne, proved to be well fortified and easy to defend and therefore excellently suited for a viking stronghold. When no show of arms was sufficient to rout the Northmen from Angers, the Franks and the Bretons conceived the idea of changing the route of the river so as to place the viking ships on dry land. The vikings realized their plight and promised under oath to depart in peace, to pay a considerable sum of money to Charles the Bald, and never to rob or to

[31] *Annales Bertiniani*, 865.

[32] *Ibid.*, 866.

[33] *Ibid.* The Northmen evidently "had reason to suspect not only the weight and fineness of the Frankish coins, but also the good faith of the Frankish officials in the process of weighing" (Joranson, *op. cit.*, p. 54, note 61).

permit robbing within his domains as long as he lived. On these conditions they were permitted to remain at Noir-moutier until the following February, " in order that they might be able to carry on peaceful trade." Their promises were secured by the handing over of pawns. But in spite of their oaths and pawns, the vikings stayed on after their time of grace had expired and occasionally made raids into the hinterland.[34]

In September of 876 more than one hundred viking ships came up the Seine. The relatively ineffective opposition offered by the rulers of the territory along the Seine was in itself an invitation to the vikings to repeat their attack. The Northmen were informed of the fact that Charles the Bald had marched toward Aix and Cologne to secure the king-dom of Louis the German, who had died in the same year. At Andernack the forces of Charles were completely routed by an army of Saxons and Thuringians,[35] and any offensive move against the Northmen was now out of question. For a consideration of 5,000 pounds of silver, " according to weight," the Northmen agreed to depart.[36] At this time an agreement was also made between the magnates of the region of the lower Loire and a viking band established there. The amount of the tribute paid is not known, but it seems prob-able that it was less than 5,000 pounds.[37]

After the death of Charles the Bald in 877, the various viking bands bought off by him returned. In July of 879 a large viking army which had found life rather dull in England crossed to Flanders. Having sacked Therouanne, they followed the Scheldt and plundered Brabrant. In November they had taken Ghent and established their head-

[34] *Annales Bertiniani*, 873.
[35] *Ibid.*, 876.
[36] *Ibid.*, 877.
[37] Joranson, *op. cit.*, p. 96, note 21 and p. 108.

quarters for the winter in that city.   It was also about this time that Northmen captured Count Eberhard of Frisia, who later was released for a high ransom.[38]   In 880 the vikings lost several thousand men in the famous battle of Saucourt, near the river Somme.[39]

In 881 Danish Northmen had established themselves at Elsloo by the Maas and from here went on excursions to Aix, Cologne, Bonn and Trier.   Having taken the city of Aachen, they used its church of St. Mary as a stable for their horses.[40]   In 882 Charles the Fat gathered a large army which met the Danes at Elsloo.   Following negotiations between Charles and the viking chieftains Godfred, Sigfred and Orm, peace was agreed upon.   Godfred received a large sum of money and was to gain complete control of the greater part of Holland, i. e., between the Vlie and the Scheldt.   In turn Godfred agreed to become baptized and to protect his grant against other vikings.[41]   This settling of Northmen in Frisia, though it anticipated the last phase of the viking aggression, namely colonization, was of short duration, lasting only four years or from 882 to 886.[42] Permanent settlements were not established until a generation later.   In 883, after only one year of occupancy, Godfred considered himself sufficiently entrenched in his province to forget his promises and permitted another viking army to pass through his domains into the adjoining region along the Rhine.   In this campaign Duisburg was captured, and when the vikings finally were forced to retreat, the town was burned.[43]   The Northmen lost a hundred or more

---

[38] *Annales Fuldenses*, 880; Steenstrup, *op. cit.*, vol. ii, p. 197.

[39] *Annales Fuldenses*, 880.

[40] *Annales Fuldenses*, 881; Steenstrup, *op. cit.*, vol. ii, p. 199.

[41] *Annales Fuldenses*, 882; *Annales Bertiniani*, 882.

[42] See *Anglo-Saxon Chron.*, 882-886.

[43] *Annales Fuldenses*, 884.

men in this encounter, which was their last in the upper Rhine region.

When Godfred found that his province provided insufficient quantities of wine for his men, he threatened to break the peace with Charles the Fat unless the latter gave him also Coblenz, Andernach and a few other wine-producing districts.[44] Charles contrived to have Godfred killed, and his followers were soon annihilated or absorbed by the other war-lords in the Low Countries and France.

In 882 Godfred and Sigfred had plundered and laid waste virtually every place of importance in the territory comprising the valleys of the lower Rhine, the Meuse and the Scheldt. Most of the inhabitants, the clergy in particular, had fled before the devastation.[45] After several unsuccessful attempts by the East Franks to check the invaders, it was finally agreed that the vikings should cease their operations in the East Frankish kingdom during the life-time of Charles upon the payment of 2,412 pounds of gold and silver to the vikings. Godfred was to become a Christian and accept baptism. Two hundred ships laden with booty were sent home, while the vikings themselves went into the neighboring kingdom of the West Franks to continue their operations.[46] Later Sigfred and Orm established themselves in the Cloister of Conde in Hennegan, within the domains of Carleman. From here they harried in Flanders, Brabant and Picardy. The Northmen continued to capture and slay the Christians, to demolish the churches, and to burn the cities; in the winter of 883-884, the entire region between the Somme and the Seine was laid waste. Carloman was forced to resort to the method employed by Charles the Bald; namely, to offer silver to the enemy. The vikings

[44] Steenstrup, *op. cit.*, vol. i, p. 185.
[45] Joranson, *op. cit.*, p. 240.
[46] *Annales Fuldenses*, 882.

demanded "12,000 pounds of pure and tested silver according to the Northmen's weight," the largest tribute ever heard of up to this time.   The collecting of this fabulous sum had to be extended over a period of seven months, and " it may be taken for granted that the tax fell, as usual, on that part of the population which was least able to pay; in other words, that the holders of *mansi*,[47] together with priests and merchants, were forced to pay not only what might be regarded as their legitimate share, but also that additional amount which, in justice, ought to have been contributed by their segniors." [48]   In November of 884, the Northmen left a barren country; some went to England, others to the kingdom of the East Franks, where they chose Louvain for their winter headquarters.

In 884, after Carloman had been accidentally killed while hunting, the vikings went against Charles the Fat who, upon the death of Carloman, had become the king also of the West Franks.   From him they demanded another 12,000 pounds of silver.[49]   Since he was unable to pay, the vikings began to plunder, and in the spring of 885 they captured Rouen.   After a series of encounters, the Northmen with a fleet of 700 larger ships and many smaller ones reached Paris in November.   Then followed the memorable siege of Paris.[50]

The vikings desired to pass through the city of Paris in order to pillage up the Seine, but the leaders of Paris refused to grant the request.   During the winter of 885-886 a hard struggle was fought over the possession of Paris.   Using

[47] A *mansus* was an estate or a farm, not exceeding twelve acres in area (Du Canze, *Glossary of Medieval Latin*).

[48] Joranson, *op. cit.*, p. 134.

[49] *Annales Fuldenses*, 884; Vogel, *op. cit.*, pp. 318-319; Joranson (*op. cit.*, p. 137) doubts that a second 12,000 pounds was ever demanded.

[50] For an account of the siege of Paris, see Kendrick, *op. cit.*, p. 215.

many devices, the vikings unsuccessfully attacked time and again. In February, 886, when their position began to weaken, the Parisians bought off Sigfred with the paltry sum of sixty pounds of silver; but the other viking chieftains continued the siege. The Franks held the city and finally, after much hesitation, Charles the Fat arrived with aid. But instead of striking a decisive blow at the Northmen, he offered them money for their departure. Since the army of Charles, to all appearances, was sufficiently strong to rout the war-worn vikings, had an earnest attempt been made, this course of action seems difficult to understand.[51]

The vikings received permission to advance up the Seine to Burgundy, where they intended to plunder during the following winter. In addition Charles promised to pay them 700 pounds of silver the following spring. The vikings had thus attained more than they first demanded.

The people of Paris and their leaders, on the other hand, showed a plucky spirit. Disregarding the agreement, they refused to permit the vikings to sail through their city, and as a result the vikings were compelled to drag their ships overland to the Seine on the other side of the city.[52] In Burgundy, a rich country heretofore virtually untouched by the vikings, these Northmen carried on their traditional activity of plundering, burning and killing. The fact that Paris itself was spared cannot be ascribed to the agreement, but to " the valor and endurance of its defenders." [53] Burgundy was made practically a wilderness by the following spring.

Most students of the viking operations in France have come to the conclusion that " if the Franks had set aside their selfish, personal interests, and had patriotically united

[51] See Joranson, *op. cit.*, p. 146, and the references listed there.
[52] Kendrick, *op. cit.*, p. 218.
[53] Joranson, *op. cit.*, p. 152, note 83.

their efforts in defense of their land and their possessions, they would in the end have prevailed over the vikings." The weakness lay not so much with the kings as with " the perverse character of the West Frankish nobility," whose " increasing greed and selfishness " and " declining, if not utter lack of patriotism " the viking leaders were not slow to utilize.[54] " Payment of Danegeld was, with the nobles, the preferred method of securing the removal of the vikings. By this expedient the magnates, in the first place, escaped all danger and all expense; for if to raise the tribute, taxes were levied also on demesnial holdings, these taxes could easily be shifted to the peasantry. Furthermore, in collecting the taxes due from their dependents, the magnates were able to reap a considerable harvest for themselves." [55]

In the spring of 887 the vikings returned to Paris to collect the 700 pounds of silver which was due. They received the money but refused to leave. An armed struggle ensued. The vikings turned towards the Marne and established themselves in a fortified camp at Chessy, not far from Meaux. They spent the winter plundering and devastating in Champagne and northern Normandy. In 888 they sacked Meaux and attacked several other towns. Odo, the new king, collected an army to protect Paris. Leaving Paris alone, the vikings centered their activities in Neustria, Burgundy and Aquitaine. In 889 Odo, at the head of an army of Franks, Aquitainians and Burgundians, met the vikings in an armed encounter. After very little fighting, payment of a sum of money to the vikings was agreed upon. The amount is not known.[56] In 892, as a result of the severe famine, the Northmen left for England, where they fought against Alfred the Great for three years.

[54] *Ibid.*, p. 128.
[55] *Ibid.*, p. 115.
[56] *Ibid.*, pp. 153-157.

In the closing years of the ninth century, a new campaign was launched on the Continent. The viking force which Alfred the Great in 896 had driven out of Mercia had gone back to the Seine country, and there followed fifteen years of irregular attacks and minor expeditions. In 897 Odo was compelled to pay a second Danegeld of an unknown amount.[57] In the years that followed, the rulers of the Franks tried to drive out the vikings but they were no more successful than the previous rulers. Finally, Charles the Simple conceived the idea of making peace with the Northmen in a way that involved neither combat nor the payment of a tribute in cash. He offered Rollo,[58] the viking leader, a part of the territory which later became known as the province of Normandy, as a fief, on the condition that Rollo embraced Christianity and paid homage to Charles. Rollo accepted these terms. The legend has it that Rollo placed his hands between the hands of Charles, which was the feudal fashion of doing homage for a fief. This was something " neither his father, nor his grandfather, nor his great-grand-father before him had ever done for any man." The legend further states that Rollo refused to kiss the king's foot, and when one of his companions was told to do it for him, the latter lifted the king's foot so high and clumsily that the king was overturned; all of which caused great amusement among the assembled Northmen.[59]

This marks the beginning of Normandy, founded in 911, as well as the end of viking attacks of major importance in this region. Thus, in the Carolingian Empire also, the

[57] *Ibid.*, pp. 158-162.

[58] Attempts have been made to show that Rollo was a Norwegian a Dane and a Swede. Although not conclusively proven, it seems as if the Norwegians had the best claims. For a summary of the debate over the nationality of Rollo, see H. Prentout, *Essai sur origines et la fondation du Duche de Normandie* (Paris, 1911), p. 153 *et seq.*

[59] C. H. Haskins, *Normans in European History* (Boston, 1915), p. 27.

viking enterprises had reached their last phase; namely, that of colonization.   Here as elsewhere, upon assuming responsibility for the safety of their region of occupancy, the Northmen gradually ceased to engage in their traditional harrying.

In other parts of the Empire, vikings continued their marauding operations.   Two more Danegelds were paid, one in 924 and the other in 926.   The former may have been quite large, for it was raised by a general tax levied throughout Francia.   The latter, raised in both Francia and Burgundy, was the last payment of which there is any record.[60]   Nantes, Angers, Tours and Orleans were again sacked; but with the recapture of Nantes in 937 by Alan Bartetorte, the viking menace was no longer a real danger even in the lower Loire region.   The victory of the Bretons over the Normans two years later marked the end of the Norman insurrection, and from then onward all Francia was free from viking attacks.

The first Danegeld on the Continent was paid in Frisia in 810, four years before the death of Charlemagne.   The amount is not known.   There were subsequent payments in 836, 837, 846 and 852.   These early tributes were all " distinctly local in character " and had not been sanctioned by the king or ruler who at the time was vested with sovereign authority in Frisia.[61]   In this respect " the Frisian Danegeld differed both from the West Frankish and the English Danegelds, which, whether tributary or stipendiary, were always paid by, or in the name of, the monarch."   Between 845 and 926 there were twelve or thirteen payments of general Danegeld, i. e., paid by the rulers or on their behalf.[62]   Since the exact amounts are given only on seven occasions, the total sum of money involved cannot be definitely stated.   The

[60] Joranson, *op. cit.*, pp. 169, 173.

[61] See *supra*, p. 123.

[62] Joranson, *op. cit.*, pp. 237, 16.

seven known tributes were paid as follows: 7,000 pounds in 845, 5,000 in 861, 6,000 in 862, 4,000 in 866, 5,000 in 877 (to the Seine vikings), 2,412 in 882 (to Godfred), 12,000 in 884, and 700 in 886. The aggregate sum is 42,112 pounds; "perhaps the remaining payments would at least double that figure and possibly triple it." The amounts paid in local Danegeld and for ransom are not ascertainable.[63] The last tribute paid by the crown was in 926, but local assessments might well have been made even after that date, although the records are silent on this point. On the whole, the tributes were smaller on the Continent than in England, but it is found that the earlier levies in England, which, roughly speaking, were contemporary with those of France, were no higher than those of the latter country.[64] There "scarcely can be any doubt that the invaders secured more treasure through plunder than through the payment of tribute."[65] Such were the viking operations in the Carolingian Empire.

[63] *Ibid.*, p. 216.
[64] *Ibid.*, p. 15.
[65] *Ibid.*, p. 217.

CHAPTER IX

SUMMARY

THE material structure of society in the North before and during the viking period rested upon the cultivation of the soil. Supplementing agriculture as a source of livelihood were fishing, hunting, and trade and piracy. In addition, the Northmen had for centuries launched occasional predatory raids as well as campaigns of prolonged warfare in foreign lands. But, although warfare had been a rather common source of livelihood in the North even prior to the viking period, the advent of the viking age inaugurated a marked shift in emphasis, and marauding as an occupation became more prominent than ever before.

In some cases there was a connection between the political unrest in the North and the viking aggression abroad, but on a larger canvas this connection appears to have been largely incidental. A number of viking leaders, like Ganger-Rolf for instance, were exiles who were very active both in the West and in the North itself, against the rulers; but these leaders were exceptions and their transactions of relatively slight consequence. Although political ambitions appear to have been partly responsible for the earlier hostilities between the Danes and the Carolingians, in the long run economic considerations were paramount. The collectors of more than 40,000 pounds in less than twenty years were little concerned over the political boundaries.[1] Seldom, and for

[1] This is the aggregate sum of the known payments, but the total returns from the campaigns in the Carolingian kingdom were doubtless several times larger. See *supra*, pp. 138-139.

the most part only toward the end of the viking period, were viking ventures " engineered, equipped and controlled by kings of Norway, Sweden and Denmark." [2] Indeed, the northern rulers " were more often embarrassed than gratified by the surprising exploits of their countrymen " in the lands across the sea.[3]

The vikings were primarily " appropriators " or rather " expropriators." [4] The Asa-religion constituted no bar to their enterprises.[5] It considered aggression not only permissible but also desirable. Only those who had fallen in battle or from wounds were worthy of entering Valhalla to participate in the never-ceasing fighting and feasting, and to be waited upon by the beautiful Valkyries. " Laughing shall I die," the ancient skald makes Ragnar Lodbrok sing.[6]

Of no small importance in the growth of the viking enterprises were the strides made in seamanship and technique of shipbuilding. Though generally undecked, the viking ships were " seaworthy enough to traverse regularly that most stormy ocean between Norway, Greenland and America." The mariners who sailed them, though without a single instrument of navigation, found a sufficient guide in the sea and sky.[7]

[2] Kendrick, *op. cit.*, p. 7.

[3] *Ibid.*, p. 18.

[4] Gustav Storm, *Kritiske bidrag til Vikingetidens historie*, p. 26.

[5] Christianity rested but lightly on the shoulders of the vikings. Even long after the Northmen had accepted the Christian faith, many of them continued to drink toasts to Christ and the Apostles with the same vigor that they formerly had toasted to Odin and Thor. Hincmar (*Annales Bertiniani*) states that in 876 several Northmen were baptized and brought before Charles the Bald, who "rewarded them generously, but they continued to live like heathens."

[6] Rudolf Keyser, *The Religion of the Northmen* (New York, 1854), p. 167.

[7] S. C. Gilfillan, *op. cit.*, p. 48.

In its effect, the viking aggression had much in common with the great migrations that took place a few centuries earlier, and in relation to the larger history of the world, the viking unrest may well be considered as one of the movements in which later developments in Europe had their inception. The viking enterprises brought Nordic blood and institutions to many parts of Europe and helped to establish new political units, notably the Russian principalities and, in a measure, Normandy. But while the viking movement may in some respects resemble the *Völkerwanderungen,* there were nevertheless marked differences between the two phenomena. In the great migrations the peoples moved *en masse* from one habitat to another, and the abandoned region remained without a population until the arrival of other tribes. The viking enterprises consisted of many individual ventures, directed at several regions and pursued with varied degrees of intensity from year to year for more than two centuries. The primary purpose of the participants was not to settle down permanently in the region to which they came, nor to establish colonies. With the exception of the settling of Iceland and some of the islands off Scotland, colonization was not a matter of predetermined policy. The viking enterprises were originally based upon individual initiative, and the aim was to secure immediate material gain, either by piracy, trade and raids on foreign shores, by exacting taxes or tributes, or by serving as mercenaries in the employ of foreign potentates. While a certain part of the population emigrated, the great majority remained at home. Both warrior and merchant vikings generally retained their headquarters in the North, even though their activities took them to distant places.

The many-sidedness of the viking activities reflects the Northmen's ability to adapt themselves to the different conditions in the various regions to which they came, as well as to the changes brought about in the course of time in the same region. Thus, the greater emphasis placed upon trade in the operations in Russia came more as a result of the environmental factors than from a proclivity to trade on the part of the Swedish vikings. Considerable changes occurred even at this early time in every one of the regions to which the vikings came during two centuries and a half. During this long period the viking activities underwent an evolution from a rather inconspicuous beginning as piracy and occasional raiding on land to military operations of international consequence, as demonstrated by the viking power in Kiev, England and Normandy. For a time England was ruled by Danish kings, Ireland by Norwegians and Russia by men from Sweden. With increasingly stronger opposition abroad, consolidations and mergers within the ranks of the viking leaders became more frequent. This trend toward monopolistic practices in turn made the viking enterprises, in their chief forms of marauding and warfare, less remunerative to the individual participants. The activities having expanded until they reached a point which called for concerted action on the part of the promoters, the latter were forced to take a hand in the administration of the various regions that constituted their " markets " in order to safeguard their interests, or more specifically, in order that they might retain their power of collecting tributes. This entailed a number of problems which only a king or a leader possessing a military organization could cope with successfully. In this new order, the " little fellow " had no place. On the surface, the ceding of Normandy to the Northmen may seem to be somewhat different from the conquests in England and Ireland, but fundamentally the development was very much the same.

There were periods during which viking activity was greater and the returns higher than at other times. When there were strong leaders in England, Ireland and the Carolingian Empire, the profits from the viking enterprises fell off markedly, and, as a result, fewer " deals " were attempted or contemplated. But as soon as the opposition again became weak, the vikings were on hand to make the most of the situation.

In addition to the more or less official payments made by the rulers of the harassed lands to the various viking leaders, there were necessarily innumerable other " takings " of which there are no or only fragmentary records in existence. It is quite impossible to give figures for the returns of the activities in Ireland, Russia and some of the other fields. Furthermore, in order fully to appreciate the value of the payments of which the annals tell, it would be necessary to translate the sums involved into terms of purchasing power of the present era, a task of insurmountable obstacles.

The viking activities dominated an epoch in the history of the North. But times changed. Like any other form of human enterprise, the traffic ran its course and was discontinued when it ceased to be profitable. The rulers across the seas obtained a firmer hold in their respective regions, and as time elapsed, dissension within their domains became less violent. All along the western front of viking operation, the traditional victims overcame the technological advantages of the Northmen by securing fleets with which they successfully resisted the attacks of the vikings; their forces on land were also being strengthened until they became real obstacles to the marauders from the North. In the East the contacts between the vikings in Russia, who had settled to become traders and an upper governing class, and the Swedes across the Baltic gradually lapsed, and the former resisted any advances made by their cousins of a later day. Since no honor was attached to being repelled and returning empty-handed, marauding as an occupation lost its appeal to the sons of the former vikings. In time it became distinctly out of fashion, and the warrior viking lost caste also in the North, as is suggested by a saga-quotation from the closing decades of the viking period. " Trading is now more highly spoken of," says Brynjolf to his son when the latter asked for a viking ship with which to go out on a plundering voyage.[8] But as time elapsed, the changed conditions, both in the North itself and in the traditional " markets ", caused trade to be pursued on a new basis. Fighting prowess became less important. Under the conditions that the new order imposed, most Northmen apparently lacked the qualifications for successful traders and faded out of the picture. During the viking period proper, the Frisians and the Anglo-Saxons were very active traders throughout Northwestern Europe.[9] In the years that followed, North German and Frisian merchants came to the North in increasing numbers, and whether they resided at home or in Scandinavia, they soon gained a virtual control of the commercial life of Northern Europe. They became the predominant element of the population in practically all the commercial centers of the North; Visby, at one time the foremost trading mart in the Baltic, reached its height under the influence of German traders chiefly, and became an important member of the Hanseatic League. The Northmen themselves, on the other hand, turned more to farming and allied pursuits, paying little attention to what took place outside their own immediate domains. Since there was no one handy to rob, the viking business, figuratively speaking, was reorganized, went into receivership and finally ceased to exist in the eleventh or twelfth century.

[8] *Egil's Saga*, ch. 32.
[9] See Elias Wadstein, *Norden och Västeuropa i gammal tid.*

BIBLIOGRAPHY

I. Primary Sources

Adam of Bremen, *Gesta Hammaburgensis ecclesiae pontificum*, ed. by Bernhard Schmeidler, Hanover and Leipzig, 1917.

——, . . . *för 640 åhr sedan författade beskrifning om Swerige Danmark ock Norge förswenskad af J. E. Peringskjöld*, Stockholm, 1718.

Agrip af Noregs konunga Sögur: herausgegeben von Finnur Jónsson (*Altnordische Saga-Bibliothek*, vol. 18), Halle, 1929.

Äldre Västgötalagen, see Beckman, Nat.

Alfred the Great, *A Description of Europe and the Voyages of Othere and Wulfstan*, translated by J. Bosworth, London, 1855.

Anglo-Saxon Chronicle, translated by E. E. C. Gomme, London, 1919.

Annales Fuldenses, Annales Bertiniani, Annales Vedastini and *Annales Xantenses*, in *Monumenta Germaniae Historica*, G. H. Pertz, *Scriptores*, vols. i-ii, Hanover, 1826. Translations into German are found in *Die Geschichtschreiber der deutschen Vorzeit, Zweite Gesammtausgabe neunzehn Jahrhundert*, Bd. viii.

Annals of the Kingdom of Ireland by the Four Masters, see *Four Masters*.

Annals of Ulster, ed. by W. M. Hennessy, Dublin, 1887.

Anskar, the Apostle of the North 801-865. Transl. from the *Vita Anskarii* by Bishop Rimbert his fellow missionary and successor. By Charles H. Robinson, London, 1921.

Beovulf, see Mullenhoff, Karl.

——, translated with Introduction and Notes by Archibald Strong, London, 1915.

Burnt Njal, translated by Sir G. W. Dasent, London, 1907.

Chronicon Fontanellense, in *M. G. H.*, Pertz, *Scriptores*, vol. ii.

Chronicon Scotorum, A Chronicle of Irish Affairs from the Earliest Times to A. D. 1135. Edited with translation by W. M. Hennessy, Rolls Series, London, 1866.

Constantin Porphyrogenitus, *De Administrando imperio*, Bonn, 1840.

——, *De Cerimona*, Bonn, 1829.

Corpus Poeticum Boreale; the Poetry of the Old Northern Tongue, From the Earliest Times to the Thirteenth Century. Edited, classified and translated with Introduction, Excursus and Notes by Gudbrand Vigfusson and F. York Powell, Oxford, 1883.

146

Edda Sæmundur (*The Poetic Edda*), translated with an Introduction and Explanatory Notes by Lee M. Hollander, Austin, 1928. See also *Prose Edda*.

Einhard, *Einhard's Life of Charlemagne*, edited, with Introduction and Notes by H. W. Garrod and R. B. Mowat, Oxford, 1915.

——, *Einhard and the Monk of St. Gall: Early Lives of Charlemagne*, translated and edited by A. J. Grant, London, 1926.

Einhardi Annales, in *M. G. H.*, Pertz, *Scriptores*, vol. ii.

Egil's Saga, translated by E. R. Eddison, Cambridge, 1930.

Eyrbyggjasaga, contained in *Origines Islandicae*, vol. ii.

Flateyjarbok, with an Introduction by Finnur Jonsson, London, 1930.

Færeyinga Saga, The Saga of the Faroe Islanders, translated by M. A. C. Press, with an Introduction by E. E. Kellet, London, 1934.

Fornsogur, ed. by G. Vigfusson and T. Mobius, Leipzig, 1864.

Fostbrædra Saga, contained in F. Winkel-Horn, *Billeder af Livet paa Island*, Copenhagen, 1871-1876.

Four Masters, Annals of the Kingdom of Ireland by the Four Masters, edited with Translation and Notes by W. M. Hennessy, Dublin, 1887.

Frostathings Law, translated by L. M. Larson, in *The Earliest Norwegian Laws*, New York, 1935.

Gesta Danorum, see *Saxo Grammaticus*.

Gesta Hammaburgensis ecclesiae pontificum, see Adam of Bremen.

Grágás, Islændernes Lovbog i Fristatens Tid, Udgivet efter det Kongl. Bibliotheks Haandskrift og oversat af Vilhjalmur Finsen, Copenhagen, 1852-1870.

Gulathings Law, translated by L. M. Larson, in *The Earliest Norwegian Laws*, New York, 1935.

Gunnlaug Serpents Tongue, The Story of Gunnlaug the Worm-tongue and Raven the Skald, London, 1896.

Guta Lag och Guta Saga, edited by Hugo Popping, Copenhagen, 1905-1907.

Hacon, The Saga of Hacon and a Fragment of the Saga of Magnus, translated by Sir G. W. Dasent, Rolls Series, London, 1894.

Heimskringla, edited by E. Monsen, translated into English with the Assistance of E. Smith, Cambridge, 1932.

Hrafnkels saga Freysgoda, edited with Introduction and Glossary by Stanton Cawley, Cambridge, 1932.

Ibn Fadlan (Ashmed), "Ibn Fadlan's Account of Scandinavian Merchants on the Volga in 922," transl. by A. S. Cook, *The Journal of English and Germanic Philology*, vol. xxii (1923).

Ingvar Vittfarnes Saga, translated by N. R. Brocman, Stockholm, 1762.

Islendingabók (*The Book of the Icelanders*) by Ari Thorgilsson, edited and translated with an introductory essay and notes by Halldor Hermannsson, *Islandica*, vol. xx, Ithaca, 1930.

Jomsvikingasagan, Utgiven af Gustaf Cederschiöld, Lund, 1862.

Jordanes (Jornandes), *The Gothic History of Jordanes,* in English version, with an Introduction and a Commentary by C. C. Mierow, Princeton, 1915.

King's Mirror, translated from Old Norwegian by L. M. Larson, New York, 1917.

Knytlinga Saga, in *Saga Bibliothek,* vol. iii.

Landnámabók, The Book of the Settlement of Iceland, translated from the Original Icelandic of Ari the Learned by Rev. T. Ellwood, Kendal, 1908.

Liudprand, °*The Works of Liudprand and Cremona,* translated with an Introduction by F. A. Wright, London, 1930.

Life of Anskar, see *Anskar.*

Laxdaela Saga, translated by Thorstein Veblen, New York, 1925.

Monumenta Historica Norvegiae, Latinske kildeskrifter til Norges historie i middelalderen, Undgivne ved G. Storm, Oslo, 1880.

Njal, see *Burnt Njal.*

Nestor, see *Russian Primary Chronicle.*

Norges Gamle Love indtil 1387, ed. by R. Keyser and P. A. Munch, Oslo, 1846.

Novgorod Chronicle: 1016-1417, translated into English by Robert Michell and Nevill Forbes, Camden Third Series, Royal Hist. Society, vol. xxv (London, 1914).

Ordericus Vitalis, *The Ecclesiastical History of England and Normandy,* translated with Notes by Thomas Forester, London, 1852, vol. i.

Origines Islandicae: A collection of the More Important Sagas and other native writings relating to the settlement and Early Hist. of Iceland, edited and translated by Gudbrand Vigfusson and F. York Powell, Oxford, 1905.

Orkneyingers' Saga, translated by Sir G. W. Dasent, Rolls Series, London, 1894.

Prose Edda, translated by A. E. Brodeur, New York, 1916.

Rimbert, see *Anskar.*

Russian Primary Chronicle, translated with Introduction by Samuel H. Cross, *Harvard Studies and Notes in Philology and Literature,* vol. xxii (1930).

Saga Library, translated and edited by Wm. Morris and Eirikr Magnusson, London, 1891-1905.

Saga of the Faroe Islanders, see *Fareyinga Saga.*

Samling af Sweriges gamla lagar, ed. by H. S. Collin and C. J. Schlyter. Vols. i-ii, ed. by Collin and Schlyter, vols. iii-xiii by Schlyter alone, Stockholm, 1827-1877.

Saxo Grammaticus, *The First Nine Books of the Danish History,* trans. by Oliver Elton, with Commentary by F. York Powell, London, 1894.

——, *Sakses Danesaga*, translated by J. Olrik, Copenhagen, 1925.

Simeon of Durham, *The Historical Works of Simeon of Durham*, translated by Joseph Stevenson, London, 1855.

Sturlunga Saga, including the Islendinga Saga of Lawman Sturla Thordrson and other works, edited with Prolegomena, Appendices, Tables, Indices, and Maps by Gudbrand Vigfusson, Oxford, 1878.

Sverris saga, The Saga of King Sverri of Norway, translated by Joseph Sephton, London, 1899.

Tacitus, Cornelius, *The Works of Tacitus*, The Oxford Translation, revised, vol. ii, London, 1854.

Three Fragments of Irish Annals, edited by J. O'Donovan, Dublin, 1860.

War of the Gaedhil with the Gaill, or the Invasion of Ireland by the Danes and other Norsemen, edited with translation by J. H. Todd, Rolls Series, London, 1867.

William of Malmesbury, *Chronicle of the Kings of England*, translated by J. A. Giles, London, 1847.

II. Secondary Works

Arbman, Holger and Stenberger, Mårten, *Vikingar i Västerled*, Stockholm, 1935.

Arne, T. J., "*Sveriges förbindelser med Östern under vikingatiden*," *Fornvännen*, 1911.

——, *Det stora Svitjod*, Stockholm, 1914.

——, *La Suede et l'Orient (Arch. D'Etudes Orientales*, vol. 8), Uppsala, 1914.

——, "*Östeuropas och Nordbalkans förhistoria*," in *De forhistoriske tider i Europa*, ed. by Knud Friis Johansen, Copenhagen, 1927.

——, "*Gotländska silverfynd från vikingatiden*," *Fornvännen*, 1911.

——, "*Svenska vikingaspår i Ryssland*," *Riksföreningen för svenskhetens bevarande i utlandet, Årsbok 1932*, Gothenburg.

——, "*Rus' erövring av Berda'a år 943*," *Fornvännen*, 1932.

Arup, Erik, *Danmarks Historie*, vol. i, Copenhagen, 1925.

Aspelin, J. R., "*Erik Emundsson i Österled och ryska rikets grundläggning*," *Opuscula archaeologica Oscari Montelio Septuagenario dictata*, Stockholm, 1913.

Beckman, Nat., "*Torgny Lagman*," *Edda*, vol. 9 (1918).

——, *Äldre Västgötalagen översatt och förklarad*, Uppsala, 1924.

Belaiew, N. T., "*Frisia and its Relations with England and the Baltic Littoral in the Dark Ages*," *Journal of the British Archaeological Association*, vol. 33, part ii (1931).

Bolin, Sture, "*Birkas undergång*," *Scandia*, vol. 4 (1933).

——, "*Vikingatåg*," in *Nordisk Familjebok*, Stockholm, 1934.

Bossinnade, P., *Life and Work in Medieval Europe*, transl. by Eileen Powell, London, 1927.

Brate, Erik, in collaboration with Sophus Bugge, "*Runverser,*" *Antiqvarisk tidskrift för Sverige,* vol. 10 (1887-1891).

Bring, E. B., *Om de fordna Skandinavernas näringsfång och hushållning,* Lund, 1833.

Bryce, James, *Studies in History and Jurisprudence,* vol. i, Oxford, 1901.

Brøgger, A. W. and others, *Osebergsfundet,* Oslo, 1917-1928.

Brøgger, A. W., "The Oseberg Ship," *Saga Book of the Viking Club,* London, vol. 10 (1919).

———, *Ancient Emigrants: A History of the Norse Settlements in Scotland,* Oxford, 1929.

Bugge, Alexander, *Studier over norske byers selvstyre og handel for Hanseaternes tid,* Oslo, 1899.

———, "Contributions to the History of the Norsemen in Ireland," *Videnskabsselskabets skrifter, II Histo.-filos. Klasse, 1900,* Oslo, 1901.

———, *Nordisk sprog og nordisk Nationalitet i Irland,* Copenhagen, 1901.

———, *Vikingerne,* Oslo, 1904 and 1906.

———, *Vesterlandenes indflydelse paa nordboernes og særlig nordmændenes ydre Kultur, Levesæt, og Samfundsforhold i Vikingetiden,* Oslo, 1905.

———, "*Novgorod som varjansk By,*" *Nordisk Tidskrift,* 1906.

———, "*Die Nordeuropäischen Verkehrswege im frülen Mittelalter und die Bedeutung der Wikinger für die Entwicklung des europaischen Handels und der europäischen Schiffahrt,*" *Vierteljahrsschift für Sozial- und Wirtschaftsgeschichte,* iv (1906).

———, "Seafaring and Shipping during the Viking Ages," *Saga Book of the Viking Club,* London, vol. 6 (1908).

———, *Norges Historie,* parts i-ii, Oslo, 1909-1910.

———, "*Handel (Nordischer),*" Joh. Hoops' *Reallexikon der germanische Altertumskunde,* Strassburg, 1911-.

———, "*Nordmændernes vikingefærder i det 9:de arh. og. grundlæggelsen av hertigdommet Normandie,*" *Nordisk Tidskrift,* 1911.

———, *Den norske sjøfarts historie,* vol. i, Oslo, 1923.

———, *Den norske trælasthandels historie,* vol. i, Skien, 1925.

Bugge, Sophus, *The Home of the Eddic Poems, with Special Reference to the Helgi Lays,* rev. ed., translated by Wm. Henry Schofield, London, 1899.

———, "*Runverser,*" see Brate, Erik.

Bull, Edward, *Det norske folks liv og historie gjennem tidene,* vol. i, Oslo, 1929.

Cleasby, Richard and Vigfusson, Gudbrand, *An Icelandic-English Dictionary,* based on the *MSS* Collection of the late Richard Cleasby, enlarged and completed by Gudbrand Vigfusson, Oxford, 1908.

Collin, H. S., see *Samling af Sweriges gamla lagar.*

Collingwood, W. G., *Scandinavian Britain,* with Chapters Introductory to the subject by the late F. York Powell, London, 1908.

Cronholm, Abraham, *Fornnordiska Minnen*, Lund, 1833-1835.

Cunningham, W., *Growth of English Industry and Commerce*, vol. i, Cambridge, 1922.

Dasent, G. W., *Introduction to the Story of Burnt Njal*, vol. i, Edinburgh, 1861.

——, *The Vikings of the Baltic* (The Story of the Jomsvikings), London, 1875.

Dorn, Bernhard, *Caspia: über die Einfülle der alten Russen in Tarbaristan, Mem. Acad. Imp. des Sciences, St. Petersburg, 8 S.* xxiii (1877).

Dreyer, W., *Nordens Oldtid*, Copenhagen, 189– (Year of publication not indicated).

Ekholm, R., "*Rus — et Varag — dans les noms de lieux de la region de Novgorod*" (*Arch. d'Etudes Orientales*, vol. ii), Uppsala, 1915.

Enander, Joh. A., *Våra fäders sinnelag: fornnordiska karaktersdrag tecknade efter den islandska sagolitteraturen*, Stockholm, 1894.

Erslev, Kr., "*Danmarks Folkemængde i Valdemar Sejrs Tid,*" *Dansk Historisk Tidsskrift*, 5 Række, 5 Bind (1885).

Falk, Hjalmar, "Altnordisches Seewesen," *Worter und Sachen, Kulturhistorische Zeitschrift für Sprach und Sachforschung*, Heidelberg, 1912.

——, *Altnordische Waffenkunde*, Oslo, 1914.

Friesen, Otto von, "*Historiska runinskrifter,*" *Fornvännen*, 1909 and 1911.

——, *Runorna i Sverige*, Uppsala, 1928.

Fors, A. P., *The Ethical World-Conception of the Norse People*, Chicago, 1904.

Gathorne-Hardy, G. M., *Norway*, London, 1925.

Geijer, Erik Gustav, *Samlade skrifter*, vol. i, Stockholm, 1851.

Gilfillan, S. C., *Inventing the Ship*, Chicago, 1935.

Gjerset, Knut, *A History of the Norwegian People*, vol. i, New York, 1915.

——, *A History of Iceland*, London, 1924.

Gjessing, A., "*Trældom i Norge,*" *Annaler for nordisk Oldkyndighed og Historie*, Copenhagen, 1862.

Gjessing, G., "*Norske og fremmede sverd i vikingetiden,*" *Norsk Historisk Tidsskrift*, 5 Række, 8 Bind (1931).

Green, J. R., *The Conquest of England*, New York, 1883.

Grimberg, Carl, *Svenska folkets underbara öden*, vol. i, Stockholm, 1926.

Grönbeck, Vilhelm, *Vor Folkeæt i Oldtiden*, Copenhagen, 1909.

Gross, Charles, *The Gild Merchant*, Oxford, 1890.

Gudmundsson, Valtyr, *Nordboernes Skibe i Vikinge- og Sagatiden*, Copenhagen, 1900.

——, "*Ackerbau (Norden),*" in Joh. Hoops' *Reallexikon*.

——, *Island i Fristatstiden*, Copenhagen, 1924.

Gustafson, Gabriel, "Notes of a Decorated Bucket from the Oseberg Find," *Saga Book of the Viking Club*, London, vol. 5 (1907).

Haliday, C., *The Scandinavian Kingdom of Dublin*, Dublin, 1884.

Hälsingborgs historia, vol. i, edited by L. M. Bååth, Hälsingborg, 1925.

Hansen, A. M., *Oldtidens Nordmænd; Opgav og Bosætning*, Oslo, 1907.

Haskins, C. H., *The Normans in European History*, Boston, 1915.

Hermannsson, Halldor, "The Ancient Laws of Norway and Iceland," *Icelandica*, vol. iv, Ithaca, 1911.

——, "Introductory Essay, the Book of the Icelanders (*Islendingabók*)," *Islandica*, vol. xx, Ithaca, 1930.

——, "The Winland Voyages," *The Geographical Review*, vol. xvii (1927).

Hertzberg, Ebbe, *En fremstilling af det norske aristokratis historie indtil kong Sverres tid*, Oslo, 1869.

Hickey, Emily M., "The Battle of Maldon," *Verse-Tales, Lyrics, and Translation*, London, 1889.

Hildebrand, Hans, *Sveriges Medeltid; kulturhistorisk skildring*, Stockholm, 1879-1903.

——, "De öster- och västerländska mynten i Sveriges jord," in *Festskrift tillägnad C. G. Malmström*, Stockholm, 1897.

Holmberg, A. E., *Nordbon under hednatiden*, Stockholm, 1852.

Hovgaard, William, *Voyages of the Norsemen to America*, New York, 1914.

Hull, Elinor, "The Gael and the Gall," *Saga Book of the Viking Club*, London, vol. 5 (1907).

Jaakkola, Jalmari, "*Findlands handel och sjöfart under tidigare medeltiden*," in *Nordisk Kultur*, vol. 16, Stockholm, 1933.

Jacobsen, L., *Svenskevældets Fald*, Copenhagen, 1929.

Johnson, Oscar Albert, "*Norges handel og Skibsfart i Middelalderen*," in *Nordisk Kultur*, vol. 16, Stockholm, 1932.

Jonsson, Finnur, *Den oldnorske og islandske Litteraturs Historie*, Copenhagen, 1894-1902.

Joranson, Einar, *The Danegeld in France, Augustana College Library Publications no. 10*, Rock Island, 1923.

Keary, C. F., *The Vikings in Western Christendom*, London, 1891.

Kendrick, T. D., *A History of the Vikings*, London, 1911.

Keyser, Rudolf, *Efterladte Skrifter*, Oslo, 1866-1867.

——, *The Religion of the Northmen*, New York, 1854.

Kluychevsky, V. O., *A History of Russia*, vol. i, translated by C. H. Hogarth, London, 1911.

Koht, Halvdan, *Innhogg og utsyn i norsk historie*, Oslo, 1921.

——, "The Scandinavian Kingdoms until the End of the Thirteenth Century," *Cambridge Medieval History*, vol. 6, ch. ix (1929).

Konig, Ed., "*Zur Vorgeschichte des Namens 'Russen',*" *Zeitschrift d. deutschen morgenländischen Gesellschaft*, vol. 70 (1916).

Kulischer, I. M., *Allgemeine Wirtschaftsgeschichte des Mittelalters und der Neuzeit*, vol. i, Munich, 1928.

Laborde, E. D., " The Site of the Battle of Maldon," *English History Review*, vol. 40 (1925).

Larsen, Sofus, " *Jomsborg, dens beliggenhed og Historie*," in *Aarbøger for Nordisk Oldkyndighed og Historie*, 3 Række, 17 and 18 Bind, Copenhagen, 1927-1928.

Larson, L. M., *Canute the Great*, New York, 1912.

——, *The Earliest Norwegian Laws* (Introduction), New York, 1935.

——, " Witnesses and Oath Helpers," in *C. H. Haskin's Anniversary Essays in Medieval History*, Boston, 1929.

Leach, Henry Goddard, *Angevine Britain and Scandinavia*, Cambridge, 1921.

Lehmann, Karl, " *Kauffriede und Friedensschild*," *Germanistische Abhandlungen zum 70. Geburtstag Konrad von Maurers*, Gothingen, 1893.

Lindqvist, Sune, " *Hedeby och Birka*," *Fornvännen*, 1926.

——, " *Slesvig och Birka*," *Fornvännen*, 1926.

——, " *Sveriges handel och samfärdsel under forntiden*," in *Nordisk Kultur*, vol. 16, Stockholm, 1933.

——, *Svenskarna i heden tid*, Stockholm, 1935.

Lipson, E., *The Economic History of England*, vol. i, New York, 1929.

Lönberg, Sven Erik, *Adam af Bremen och hans skildring af nordeuropas länder och folk*, Uppsala, 1897.

London Museum Catalogues, no. 1, see Wheeler, R. E. M.

Lundbye, Peter, " *Haløre Marked*," *Dansk Hist. Tidsskrift*, 7 Række, 4 Bind (1904).

Magnusson, Eirikr, " Notes on shipbuilding and Nautical terms of Old in the North," *Saga Book of The Viking Club*, London, vol. 4 (1905).

Maitland, F. W., *Domesday and Beyond*, Cambridge, 1897.

Maurer, Konrad von, *Island von seiner ersten Entdeckung bis zum Unterganze des Freistaats*, Munich, 1874.

Mawer, Allen, *The Vikings*, Cambridge, 1913.

——, " The Vikings," *Cambridge Medieval History*, vol. 3 (1923), ch. xiii.

——, " The Viking Age," in *Travel and Travellers of the Middle Ages*, edited by A. B. Newton, London, 1926.

Meyendorff, Baron A., " Trade and Communication in Eastern Europe, A. D. 800-1200," in *Travel and Travellers of the Middle Ages*, edited by A. P. Newton, London, 1926.

Montelius, Oscar, *Sveriges hednatid, samt medeltid*, Stockholm, 1898.

——, *The Civilization of Sweden in Heathen Times*, translated by F. H. Woods, London, 1888.

——, " *Sveriges förbindelser med andra länder i förhistorisk tid*," *Festskrift tillägnad C. G. Malmström*, Stockholm, 1897.

——, " Nār kommo svenskarna till Finland? " Finsk Tidskrift, vol. 44 (1898).

——, Forntiden, Sveriges historia, ed. by E. Hildebrand, vol. i, Stockholm, 1903.

——, " Handeln i fordna dagar med sārskilt avseende på tiden före Kristi födelse," Nordisk Tidskrift, 1908.

——, " Sverige och vikingafärderna västerut," Antikvarisk Tidskrift för Sverige, vol. 21 (1919).

——, " De ariska folkens hem," Nordisk Tidskrift, 1921.

——, " Sveriges skattskyldighet under Rom," Svensk Tidskrift, 1890.

Mullenhoff, Karl, Beovulf, Berlin, 1889.

Müllenhoff, Karl and Scherer, W., Denkmäler deutscher poesie und Prosa, Berlin, 1892.

Mueller, P. E., Saga Bibliothek, Copenhagen, 1814-1820.

Muller, Sophus, Vor Oldtid, Copenhagen, 1897.

Munch, P. A., Det norske folks historie, vols. i-ii, Oslo, 1852-1853.

Munthe, Arnold, Sjömaktens inflytande på Sveriges historia, Marinlitteraturföreningens Arbeten, no. 24, Stockholm, 1922.

Nansen, Fridjof, In Northern Mists, translated by A. G. Chater, New York, 1911.

Nerman, Birger, Studier över Svärges hedna litteratur, Uppsala, 1913.

——, " Ynglingasagan i arkeologisk belysning," Fornvännen, 1917.

——, " The Foundation of the Swedish Kingdom," Saga Book of the Viking Club, London, vol. 9 (1914).

——, Det svenska rikets uppkomst, Stockholm, 1925.

——, Die Verbindungen Zwischen Skandinavien und dem Ostbaltikum in der jüngeren Eisenzeit, Kungl. Vitterh, Hist. och Antikv. Akad., Handlingar 40: 1, Stockholm, 1929.

——, En utvandring från Gotland och öns införlivande med sveaväldet, Kungl. Vitterh., Hist. o. Antikv. Akad., Handl. 34, Stockholm, 1922.

——, " Svenska vikingakolonier vid Östersjön," Nordisk Tidskrift, 1934.

Nicolaysen, N., The Viking Ship Discovered at Gökstad in Norway, Oslo, 1882.

Nihlén, Johan, Under rutat segel: svenska äventyr i öster, Stockholm, 1928.

Nordenstreng, Rolf, Vikingafärderna, Stockholm, 1926.

Nordman, C. A., " Finlands handel med Skandinavien under forntiden," in Nordisk Kultur, vol. 10, Stockholm, 1933.

Olrik, Axel, Heroic Legends of Denmark, New York, 1919.

——, Viking Civilization, New York, 1930.

Osebergsfundet, see Brøgger, A. W.

Pares, Bernard, A History of Russia, New York, 1928.

Petersen, Jan, " De norske vikingesverd," Videnskabsselskabets Skrifter, Oslo, 1919.

——, "*Vikingestudier*," *Bergens Museums Aarbok, 1919-1920*, Bergen, 1920.
——, "*Handel i Norge i Vikingetiden*," in *Nordisk Kultur*, vol. 16, Stockholm, 1933.
Phillpotts, Bertha, *Kindred and Clan in the Middle Ages and After; a study in the Sociology of the Teutonic Races*, Cambridge, 1913.
Pirenne, Henri, *Medieval Cities*, Princeton, 1925.
Plummer, Charles, *Two of the Saxon Chronicles Parallel, Notes*, vol. ii, Oxford, 1899.
——, *The Life and Times of Alfred the Great*, Oxford, 1902.
Poupardin, Ren., *The Carolingian Kingdoms, Cambridge Mediaeval History*, vol. 3, 1922, chs. ii and iii.
Pratt, Fletcher, "The Cavalry of the Vikings," *U. S. Cavalry Journal*, vol. 42 (1933).
Prentout, H., *Essai sur les origines et la fondation du Duche de Normandie*, Paris, 1911.
Raudonikas, W. J., *Die Normannen der Wikingerzeit und das Ladogagebiet, Kungl. Vitterh., Hist., och Antikv. Akad. Handlingar*, 40: 3, Stockholm, 1930.
——, "*Svenskt och finskt i Gardarike*," *Fornvännen*, 1931.
Reeve, Sidney A., *The Evolution of Social Crises: History as a Natural Phenomenon*, vol. 2, typed ms. in New York Public Library.
——, "Ships and Social Evolution," *The Geographical Review*, vol. 23 (1933).
Roos, William, "The Swedish Part in the Viking Expeditions," *Eng. Hist. Review*, vol. 7 (1892).
Rosenberg, C., *Nordboernes Aandsliv*, Copenhagen, 1880.
Runciman, Steven, *The Emperor Romanus Lecapenus and His Reign*, Cambridge, 1929.
Schlyter, C. J., see *Samling af Sweriges gamla lagar*.
Schreiner, Johan, *Olav den hellige og Norges Samling*, Oslo, 1927.
Schück, Adolf, "*Sjöborgar och hamnstäder*," *Fornvännen*, 1924.
——, *Det svenska rikets uppkomst och äldsta utveckling*, Stockholm, 1927.
Schück, Henrik, *Birka*, Uppsala, 1910.
——, *Studier i Ynglingatal*, Uppsala, 1910.
——, *Svenska folkets historia*, vol. i, Stockholm, 1914.
Seebohm, Frederic, *Tribal Custom in Anglo-Saxon*, London, 1902.
Shetelig, Haakon, "Queen Asa's Sculptors," *Saga Book of the Viking Club*, London, vol. 10 (1919).
——, *Det norske folks historie gjennem tidene*, vol. i, Oslo, 1930.
——, *Vikingeminner i Vest-Europa*, Oslo, 1933.
Smith, C. M., *Northmen of Adventure*, New York, 1931.
Sommarin, Emil, *Träldomen i Norden, Verdandi småskrifter, no. 104*, Stockholm, 1917.

Steenstrup, Japetus, "*Nogle Bemærkninger om Ottar's Beretning till Kong Alfred om Hvalros- og Hualfangst i Nordhavet paa hans tid,*" *Dansk Hist. Tidsskrift,* 6 Række, 2 Bind (1889).

Steenstrup, Joh. H. C., *Normannerne,* Copenhagen, 1876-1878.

——, *Kong Valdemars Jordebog,* Copenhagen.

——, *Venderne og de Danske for Valdemar den den Stores Tid,* Copenhagen, 1900.

——, *Normandiets Historie under de syv forste Hertuger, 911-1066,* Copenhagen, 1925.

Stefansson, Jon, "Western Influences on the Earliest Viking Settlers," *Saga Book of the Viking Club,* London, vol. 5 (1907).

——, "The Vikings in Spain," *Saga Book of the Viking Club,* London, vol. 6 (1908).

Stjerna, Knut, *Arkeologiska anteckningar till Beowulf, Kungl. Vitterh. Hist., och Antikv. Akad. Månadsblad,* Stockholm, 1903-1905.

——, "*Lund och Birka,*" *Historisk Tidskrift för Skåneland,* vol. iii, 1909.

Stomberg, A. A., *A History of Sweden,* New York, 1931.

Storm, Gustav, *Kritiske bidrag til Vikingetidens historie,* Oslo, 1878.

——, *Havelok the Dane and the Norse king Olaf Kvaran, Vidensbabsselskabets forhandlinger,* Oslo, 1879.

Strasser, K. T., *Wikinger und Normannen,* Hamburg, 1928.

Svensen, Emil, *Striden för freden,* Stockholm, 1910.

Tallgren, A. M., "*Finland vid slutet av hednatiden,*" *Fornvännen,* 1923.

Taylor, Henry Osborne, *The Medieval Mind,* vol. i, New York, 1919.

Thompson, J. W., "The Commerce of France in the Ninth Century," *Journal of Political Economy,* vol. 23 (1915).

——, *An Economic and Social History of the Middle Ages,* New York, 1928.

Thomsen, Vilhelm, *Samlede Afhandlinger,* vol. i, Copenhagen, 1919.

——, *The Relation between Ancient Russia and Scandinavia and the Origin of the Russian State,* Oxford, 1877.

Thorgilsson, Are, see *Islendingabók.*

Tunberg, Sven, *Studier rörande Skandinaviens äldsta politiska indelning,* Uppsala, 1911.

——, "*Till Svearikets äldsta historia,*" *Fornvännen,* 1920.

Vasiliev, A. A., *History of the Byzantine Empire,* vol. i, *Univ. of Wisconsin Studies in Social Science and History, no. 13,* Madison, 1928.

Vasmer, Max, *Wikingerspuren in Russland, Sitzungsberichte der Preusischen Akademie der Wissenschaften, Phil. Hist. Klasse,* vol. 24, Berlin, 1931.

Veblen, Thorstein, *Imperial Germany and the Industrial Revolution,* New York, 1918.

——, "An Early Experiment in Trusts," *The Journal of Political Economy*, vol. xii (1904), republished in *The Place of Science in Modern Civilization*, New York, 1919.

——, *The Laxdæla Saga*, with Introduction, New York, 1925.

Vedel, E., "*Bornholmske Undersøgelser med særligt Hensyn til den senere Jernalder*," *Aarbøger*, 1890.

Vigfusson, Gudbrand, "Prolegomena," *Sturlunga Saga*, vol. i, Oxford, 1878.

Velschow, H. M., "*Om Folkemængden i Denmark i det trettende aarhundrede*," *Dansk Hist. Tidsskrift*, 1 Række, 4 Bind (1843).

Visted, Kristoffer, *Vor gamle Bondekultur*, Oslo, 1908.

Vogel, Walther, *Die Normannen und das Frankische Reich bis zur Grundung der Normandie (799-911)*, Heidelberg, 1906.

——, *Geschichte der deutschen Seeschiffahrt*, Berlin, 1915.

——, "*Nordische Seefahrten in Früheren Mittelalter*," *Meereskunde I*, Heft 7.

Vogt, L. J., *Dublin som norsk by: Fra vor ældste kjøbstadsliv*, Oslo, 1896.

Vries, Jan de, *De Wikingen in de lage landen bij de Zee*, Haarlem, 1923.

Wadstein, Elis, *Norden och Vesteuropa i gammal tid*, Stockholm, 1925.

——, "Hedeby," *Fornvännen*, 1932.

Walsh, A., *Scandinavian Relations with Ireland during the Viking Period*, Dublin, 1932.

Weibull, Curt, *Sveriges och Danmarks äldsta historia*, Lund, 1922.

Weibull, Lauritz, *Kritiska undersökningar i Nordens historia omkring år 1000*, Lund, 1911.

Weinhold, Karl, *Altnordisches Leben*, Berlin, 1856.

Wergeland, Agnes M., *Slavery in Germanic Society during the Middle Ages*, Chicago, 1916.

Wheeler, R. E. M., "London and the Vikings," *London Museum Catalogues, no. 1*, London, 1927.

Williams, M. K., *Social Scandinavia in the Viking Age*, New York, 1920.

Worsaae, J. J. A., *An Account of the Danes and Norwegians in England, Scotland and Ireland*, London, 1852.

Worsaae, L. L. A., *Den Danske Erøbring af England og Normandiet*, Copenhagen, 1863.

——, *De Danskes Kultur i Vikingetiden*, Copenhagen, 1873.

——, *The Industrial Arts of Denmark from the Earliest Times to the Danish Conquest of England*, London, 1882.

——, *The Pre-History of the North*, translated by H. F. M. Simpson, London, 1886.

Zeuss, Kasper, *Die deutschen und die Nachbarstämme*, Munich, 1837.

Zimmer, Heinrich, "*Uber die frühesten Berührungen der Iren mit den Nordgermanen*," in *Zitzungsber. der. Berliner Akademie*, vol. i, Berlin, 1891.

INDEX